Scrum Project Management

Scrum Project Management

Kim H. Pries
Jon M. Quigley

CRC Press
Taylor & Francis Group
Boca Raton London New York

CRC Press is an imprint of the
Taylor & Francis Group, an **informa** business
AN AUERBACH BOOK

CRC Press
Taylor & Francis Group
6000 Broken Sound Parkway NW, Suite 300
Boca Raton, FL 33487-2742

International Standard Book Number: 978-1-4398-2515-0 (Hardback)

Library of Congress Cataloging-in-Publication Data

Pries, Kim H., 1955-
Scrum project management / Kim H. Pries, Jon M. Quigley.
p. cm.
Includes bibliographical references and index.
ISBN 978-1-4398-2515-0 (hardcover : alk. paper)
1. Agile software development. 2. Scrum (Computer software development) 3. New Products--Management. 4. Project management. I. Quigley, Jon M. II. Title.

QA76.76.D47P744 2011
005.1--dc22 2010024781

Visit the Taylor & Francis Web site at
http://www.taylorandfrancis.com

and the CRC Press Web site at
http://www.crcpress.com

Contents

List of Figures

List of Tables

Acknowledgments

We know a number of people who need to be acknowledged here.

John Wyzalek, the acquisitions editor at CRC, has been a great help with development, encouragement, and promotion of all books we have written for them.

I (Jon) would like to thank those who have contributed to refining the content and the quality of this book: Marty Foulks, Edmond Garmon, and Mike Siebert. I appreciate our many discussions about product development, philosophies, and methods. It was great kicking ideas around to improve how we get things done. This is true whether it was a waterfall discussion, scrum or other approach.

We would also like to thank the reviewers: Joakim Ringdahl and Subramanian Arumugam. We appreciate the time and effort you took in reviewing this book.

I would also like to thank Kim Pries. I learn much from our collaborations and I am ever appreciative of the opportunity to work with him.

Last but not the least, I would like to thank my family. My wife, Nancy, rocks the house, and my son, Jackson, is the best boy a daddy can have.

I (Kim) would like to thank my wife, Janise Pries, for reviewing this work—regardless, all mistakes belong to Jon and me. She is the love of my life, the reason I work such long hours to make a change in the world. I have been allowed to experiment with scrum implementations at Stoneridge Electronics–North America by Doug Marsden, Senior Director of Business Development.

We used open source tools as much as possible to help develop this book; examples are

- WinMerge (compare)
- MiKTeX (LaTeX compiler)
- TeXnicCenter (TeX-specific editor)
- Zscreen (screen capture)
- Vim (programmer's editor)

About the Authors

Kim H. ("Vajramanas") Pries has four college degrees: a BA in history from the University of Texas at El Paso (UTEP), a BS in metallurgical engineering from UTEP, an MS in metallurgical engineering from UTEP, and an MS in metallurgical engineering and materials science from Carnegie Mellon University. In addition to the degrees, he has the following certifications:

- APICS
  - Certified Production and Inventory Manager (CPIM)
- American Society for Quality (ASQ)
  - Certified Reliability Engineer (CRE)
  - Certified Quality Engineer (CQE)
  - Certified Software Quality Engineer (CSQE)
  - Certified Six Sigma Black Belt (CSSBB)
  - Certified Manager of Quality/Operational Excellence (CMQ/OE)
  - Certified Quality Auditor (CQA)

Pries has worked as a computer systems manager ("IT"), a software engineer for an electrical utility, and a scientific programmer on defense contracts. For Stoneridge, Incorporated (SRI), he has worked as

- Software manager
- Engineering services manager
- Reliability section manager
- Product integrity and reliability director

In addition to this, Pries provides Six Sigma training for both UTEP and SRI, and cost reduction initiatives for SRI. Pries is also a founding faculty member of Practical Project Management. Additionally, in concert with Jon Quigley, Pries is the co-founder and principal with Value Transformation, LLC, a training, testing, cost improvement, and product development consultancy. Pries is also a lay monk in the Soto tradition of Zen Buddhism and functions as an Ino for the Zen Center of Las Cruces. E-mail him at `kim.pries@valuetransform.com`. Pries's first book was *Six Sigma for the Next Millennium: A CSSBB Guidebook*, now in a second edition as *Six Sigma for the New Millennium: A CSSBB Guidebook, Second Edition* (ASQ Quality Press).

Jon M. Quigley has three college degrees: a BS in electronic engineering technology from the University of North Carolina at Charlotte, an MBA in marketing, and an MS in project management from City University of Seattle. In addition to the degrees, he has the following certifications:

- Project Management Institute
  - Project Management Professional (PMP)
- International Software Testing Qualifications Board (ISTQB)
  - Certified Tester Foundation Level (CTFL)

In addition to degrees and certifications, Quigley has a number of patents and awards:

- US Patent Award 6,253,131 Steering wheel electronic interface
- US Patent Award 6,130,487 Electronic interface and method for connecting the electrical systems of truck and trailer
- US Patent Award 6,828,924 Integrated vehicle communications display (also a European patent)
- US Patent Award 6,718,906 Dual scale vehicle gauge
- US Patent Award 7,512,477 Systems and methods for guiding operators to optimized engine operation
- US Patent Award 7,629,878 Measuring instrument having location controlled display
- US Published Patent Application 20090198402 Method and system for operator interface with a diesel particulate filter regeneration system
- Volvo-3P Technical Award for global IC05 Instrument cluster project 2005
- Volvo Technology Award for global IC05 Instrument cluster project April 2006

Quigley has worked in a variety of capacities within the new product development organizations:

- Embedded Product Development Engineer (hardware and software)
- Product Engineer
- Test Engineer
- Project Manager
- Electrical and Electronic Systems Manager
- Verification and Test Manager

In addition to his work at Volvo 3P in Greensboro, he is a founding member of Practical Project Management, an online project management training organization. In concert with Pries, Quigley is co-founder and principal with Value

Transformation, LLC, training, testing, cost improvement and product development consultancy. E-mail him at `jon.quigley@valuetransform.com`.

Collectively, Pries and Quigley are the authors of the books *Project Management of Complex and Embedded Systems: Ensuring Product Integrity and Program Quality*, and *Testing of Complex and Embedded Systems* (Taylor & Francis). Additionally, they have authored numerous magazine articles and presentations at product development conferences about various aspects of product development and project management.

- *Embedded Systems Design*
- *Product Design and Development*
- *Embedded Design News* (EDN)
- *Software Test and Performance* (STP)
- *Electronics Weekly* (online)
- *DSP Design Line* (online)
- *Design Reuse* (online)
- *All Business* (online)
- *Quality* magazine (online)
- *Automotive Design Line* and *Automotive Design Line Europe* (online)
- *Project Magazine* (online)
- *Tech Online India* (online)
- *Embedded Design India* (online)

Additional information about Kim Pries, Jon Quigley and Value Transformation, LLC can be found at `http://www.valuetransform.com`. There are areas to ask the authors questions and exchange ideas about product development.

Preface

Product development is becoming increasingly complex. The pace of technological change grows daily, leaving little time to accumulate expertise before development of a new product begins. Acquiring enough experience to be able to predict the risk and develop the courses of action during the development is difficult and often happens during the course of the true developmental phases of the new product development. This situation creates a need for tapping into the skills and abilities of all the participants in the development effort and relying less on heroic efforts to save the day and carry the project and product to a successful conclusion. Even when we have product development heroes and they carry the day, the loss of these individuals to the organization will be detrimental to the organization and represents a human resources risk. The recovery period can be prolonged for organizations with poor team practices and those that favor heroic actions.

We are presenting a modified version of the agile software development tool *scrum* as an alternative to traditional program management and as a tool for standard line management. Both of us have experience in deploying and implementing the tool. We understand the pitfalls of this method, which we will elucidate during the course of our discussion.

We are not saying that we believe the waterfall approach should be condemned to obscurity or that we are calling for the death of this development model. In fact, we know of few organizations that take the waterfall method as it is often portrayed in books; that is, taking it to be a rigid and one-way pass through the development process. In fact, there are some similarities between the methods, although scrum approach throughput is quicker and keeps people focused on what is deemed important by the project managers. Basically scrum is to the waterfall approach what lean manufacturing (especially one-piece flow) is to batch-mode manufacturing. Additionally, the team aspects of the method—moving toward self-directed work teams—means the actions of the team must be successful and are largely in the hands of the team itself. The concept of a self-directed work team also suggests we must have a motivated and skilled team capable of achieving project goals. It is unwise to condemn conventional tactics across the board, when frequently the conventional tactics are not executed well. Poor execution does not improve the probability of delivering a quality product no matter the model or method of execution.

We like to call this style of getting things done "high-intensity management." We demand and we see acceleration of tempo, focused completion of tasks, and improvement in project backlogs as we have never seen before. In one example, we were able to drop an automated production test equipment department's projects list from sixty items to thirty items to twenty items in less than three months! We had never been able to achieve these kinds of results until we implemented the relevant portions of the scrum approach to accomplishment. We have used the focused approach of the scrum method to drop test incident report counts from averaging approximately 110 to averaging less than 10 reports.

For some time now, organizations have tried to empower employees, sometimes as a flavor of the week exercise and sometimes with real goals in mind. Some organizations have moved to self-directed, work-based teams, which generally means pushing down much of the decision and execution of the enterprise from upstream management to downstream workers. In his book, *Leading Self-Directed Work Teams*, Kimball Fisher provides a comparative list of attributes for self-directed work teams and the traditional organization.[1] Scrum puts the control of how the product gets produced in the hands of the individuals responsible for delivery, all within the confines of the philosophies and constraints of the organization.

$$Empowerment = f\,(Authority,\ Resources,\ Information,\ Accountability)$$

$$Empowerment = 0,\ if\ Authority = 0;\ or\ Resources = 0;$$

$$or\ Information = 0;\ or\ Accountability = 0$$

Fisher takes the word "empowerment" from being a business buzzword and puts some meat on it. He also makes it clear what factors must be available for empowerment to take place.

Note

1. Kimball Fisher, *Leading Self-Directed Work Teams*, (New York, NY: McGraw Hill, 1993), 14.

Chapter 1

Why Scrum?

The scrum approach focuses on the business needs of projects when developing products and services. It provides the same benefits with line management with only minor modifications to the tools. The scrum approach strips away non-value-added activities and impels delivery by focusing on the immediate details. It is not possible to interpret scrum as anything but a disciplined development model. Its counterpart, the waterfall model, is a sequential development framework in which each major phase appears to be "pouring" its results into each successive phase. Scrum is not only iterative, but has actions that require team learning and allows the rest of the project to be built on such learning. Much team learning will occur during each cycle of the scrum activities for the project in the form of the sprint retrospective and customer planned input. Hence, we control the end game activities—the customer going directly to the developer—while still allowing the customer to make adjustments to the product as time passes. If anything, the scrum approach enhances the ability of the customer to add changes to the product.

During product development, both customer and supplier tend to acquire new knowledge about the product as they begin to implement the product specification and derived requirements. Verification and validation results may drive even more change. Both customer and developer can use the scrum approach to reduce the risk caused by midstream changes in the specification of a product.

In Kimball Fisher's book *Leading Self-Directed Work Teams*, he describes a situation facing Tektronix's that is no less applicable today:[1]

> Historically, Tek design engineers had taken about five years to develop a new product technology. As long as we could keep a product family in the marketplace for about ten years, this was not a problem. But during the 1980s, increased competition from numerous well-financed and technologically-advanced organizations changed the rule forever.

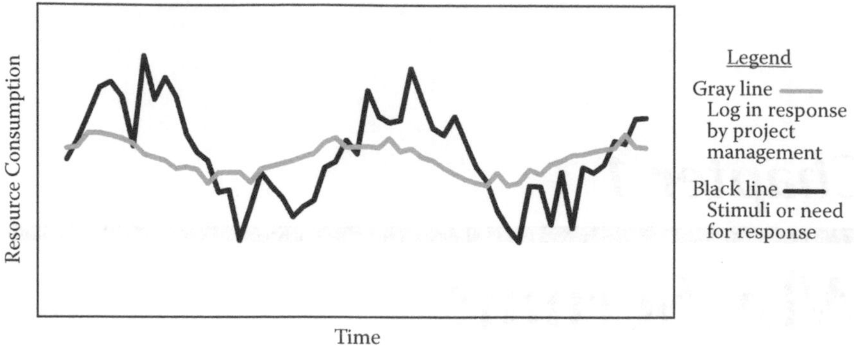

Figure 1.1 Conventional project management responses.

> Major product technologies were becoming obsolete in two years instead of ten. The technologies that new electrical and software engineers learned in school were, in fact, often obsolete twelve months after graduation . . . . Once a new technology was introduced by Tek, or by one of its able competitors, there was less than 800 days to recoup the investment and make a profit. Looked at in this light, every day of lost opportunity caused by bureaucratic slowdowns was costing the company thousands of dollars.

The pace of technological change generally accelerates, with lulls only during severe economic downturns. The ability of an organization to respond to economic variation while still delivering a quality product to schedule is valuable, perhaps more so than in previous decades. Conventional project management responses lag significantly behind the economic variation (see Figure 1.1).

The scrum approach to project management brings an exciting new dimension to the way we handle a variety of project management situations such as risk, scheduling, and other factors involved in completing a project. Scrum originated in the agile software development world and has been used primarily for software development in small- to medium-sized projects. We believe that it is time for scrum to come into its own as a tool for small- to medium-sized projects for any kind of development and for other kinds of projects; for example, Six Sigma projects. We also use the scrum approach with line management activities with one modification to the scrum tools.

Agile development, like scrum, is an instantiation of the agile manifesto (although precursors to agile development existed earlier; for example "extreme programming" or XP). This manifesto identifies key principles of operation:[2]

1. Individuals and interactions over processes and tools
2. Working software over comprehensive documentation
3. Customer collaboration over contract negotiation
4. Responding to change over following a plan

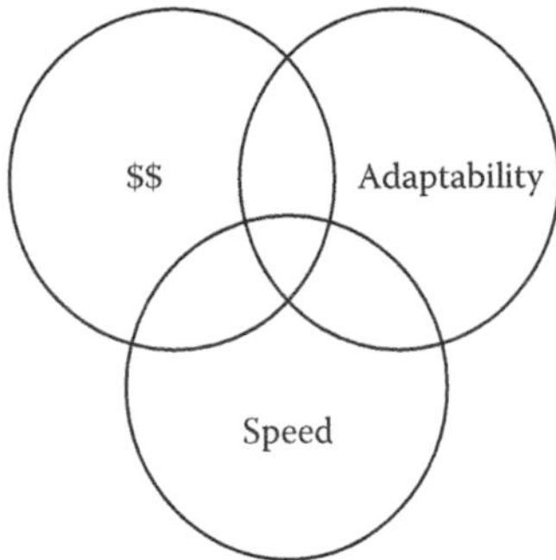

Figure 1.2 Why scrum?

According to *The Agile Customer's Toolkit* by Tom Poppendieck, agile development is centered around the seven principles of lean thinking:[3]

1. Eliminate waste—only add value, not inventory
2. Amplify learning—repeat
3. Decide as late as possible—defer commitment (note: this action is known in manufacturing as postponement)
4. Deliver as quickly as possible
5. Empower the team—train, trust, and lead
6. Build in integrity—both customer perceived and conceptual
7. See the whole—avoid suboptimizing

We prefer to think of the scrum approach that we propose as *high-intensity management*. We increase tempo, improve responsiveness, increase communications, and reduce risk. Our goal is to focus on a limited number of tasks within a short planning horizon so that we can drive them to completion and remove them from our concern. Today's product development organizations are often stretched thin in occasionally suboptimal attempts to reduce cost. Often the same human resources are used for multiple projects, which diffuses the focus of the team from a particular set of deliverables. A term that describes this behavior is "frazzing." This neologism was created by Massachusetts psychiatrist Edward Hallowell in his book *Crazy Busy: Overstretched, Overbooked, and about to Snap! Strategies for Coping in a World Gone ADD*. Frazzing is short for "frantic multitasking." While sometimes this sort of work is selected by an individual, there are times when it is thrust on him or her by the volume of actions that organizations expect the employee to execute. Scrum helps by setting a specific set of activities within a relatively short span of time; in other words, we can use scrum as a tool to convert from suboptimal multitasking to high-speed mono-tasking and get more done (see Figure 1.2).

When task load is high, it is difficult to focus on priorities. Even when we know the priorities, we sacrifice the second-level priorities which somebody in the

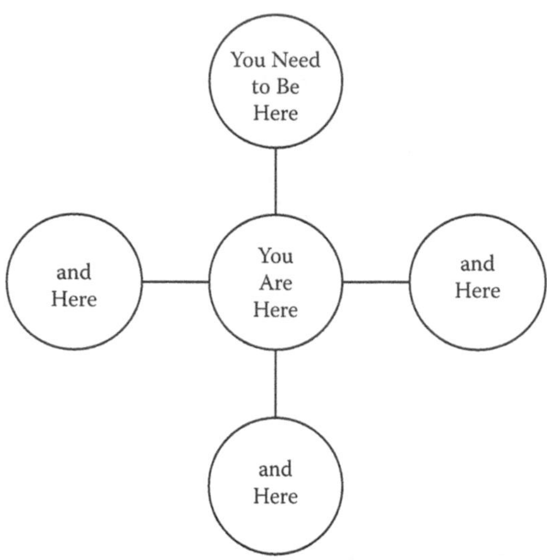

Figure 1.3 Distraction.

organization expects to be addressed. This approach can drive employees to motivational numbness such that they can't take action in any direction (see Figure 1.3).

We have implemented scrum across multiple departments and we will discuss our successes as well as some of the trials involved with the deployment of a scrum environment. Along the way, we will show you some tools you can use to make life easier. We will show you how scrum can help your project management by showing how it works in several different environments.

We will also be discussing improvisation, creative problem-solving, and emergent phenomena. One of the hallmarks of the scrum approach is the ability to adapt to reality rather than trying to force reality to adapt to our often top-heavy systems. We suggest that the scrum approach has the makings of a complex adaptive system, which provides the flexibility needed to meet shifting customer demands. We expect the scrum approach to become the preferred approach for project management and line management—an alternative to what we call "dropping the crystal." Dropping the crystal occurs when upstream managers concoct a set piece product launch process with the inflexibility implied in the phrase. These processes often have hundreds of deliverable items, tens to hundreds of controls, and obligatory marathon reviews.

It is clear from *Software Project Secrets*, by George Stepanek, why software projects differ from other sorts of projects. There are a number of attributes that make these a risky proposition:[4]

1. Software is complex.
2. Software is abstract.
3. Requirements are incomplete.
4. Technology changes rapidly.

5. Best practices are not mature (or constantly evolving).
6. Technology is a vast domain.
7. Technology experience is incomplete (segmented).
8. Software development is research.
9. Repetitive work is automated.
10. Construction is actually the design.
11. Change is considered easy (it is only software).
12. Change is inevitable.

The point behind the scrum approach is to constantly deliver a workable, sellable product to the customer at the end of each delivery period, which can be as often as each sprint. In some scenarios such as software development, this period may be as short as a day—the team executes a daily build with nightly verification of all changes plus regression testing (testing is done to see if the change has caused any problems). Daily delivery is the *ne plus ultra* of aggressive software development schedules.

This concept of planning as you go extends beyond technical projects to include business applications also. A book titled *The Plan-As-You-Go Business Plan* by Tim Berry describes the decide-and-correct approach exactly. This book illustrates the concept of just enough planning to accomplish the desired objective. The details of the objective will change as you progress through the activities, much like the learning scenario we described already.

1.1 Team!

Any discussion of scrum techniques must include the idea of the *team*, the secret weapon of scrum. The scrum approach engages people as a group and positions them to operate as a team; that is to say, a collective with goals instead of an amorphous aggregate. The team is the correct mix of stress and accomplishment, of individual effort and communal work. Beginning with team selection, scrum also provides for the removal of those individuals who are unable to contribute. For scrum, the possibility of a high-performance team starts when we state the primary common goal of our project or department.

Several years ago, we ran a project a little differently than we had in the past. We had colocated the design and testing group and had created a list of activities to produce documentation, product features, and functions as well as testing of the various items. We set this activity up in a way we refer to now as proto-scrum. The result of using this method was that far fewer resources, especially people, were required to achieve the final product, much less than the global sites that were executing the project conventionally.

Among the reasons for success included the team itself and high-speed communication channels. This group was focused on specific deliverables in a well-defined, abbreviated amount of time. While this team did not employ specific scrum tactics, they focused on a set of immediate deliverables. We saw frequent, brief discussions among the systems engineers, the development engineers, the test engineers, and the project managers. The individuals knew their individual strengths and the strengths of their teams and who was responsible for clear-cut items, such that they could keep the team progressing. These individuals were committed to their assigned deliverables and the deliverables of the team. We also saw removal of those team members who could not meet this brisk pace and intense demand.

We know from personal experience that being part of a successful team is an exciting experience. One of us had this pleasure when working on a defense contract in southern New Mexico—six of us formed an impromptu team that lasted about two years. We dragged along the other seven people on the contract, but the six of us were the driving force behind software deliveries for multiple target systems. Because the scrum approach supports small, tight teams, we have seen a similar effect with the participants in more recent venues. They begin to discuss solutions among themselves and they are gratified by the pace of accomplishment.

In his book, *Getting Things Done When You Are Not In Charge*, Geoffrey M. Bellman provides a list of his work values (see below),[5] and identifies that work that matches or supports his view. In scrum or any self-directed work team effort, we reflect on Bellman's attributes and how these apply to our teams. In the scrum scenario, we do not have a heavy-handed manager spurring on the team—the team has to figure out how to achieve its objective. While this book is not about teams as such, the team concept is key to accelerating a project to a timely completion and we will refer to the team concept frequently.

1. **Balance**. My work is in service to my larger life.
2. **Innovation**. My work feeds my need to grow and create.
3. **Authenticity**. Most often, my work encourages me to be myself rather than play a role.
4. **Contribution**. Through my work, I make a small but positive difference in the community.
5. **Courage**. I am willing to risk my standing with others to support ideas and actions.
6. **Quality**. My work standards are high; I hold myself to them.
7. **Fairness**. I judge people on their potential contribution to an investment in our work together.
8. **Trust**. I will deal with others openly and positively, and assume that I can count on them and they on me.

1.2 Agile Product/Process Development

The scrum approach originated with agile software development as practitioners looked for ways to improve communication, increase throughput, and decrease risk. The only question is why nobody generalized this approach to other forms of activity management. We are currently in an industrial environment where many

North American corporations have spent millions of dollars moving toward "lean" manufacturing. The concepts of agile and lean are closely related, with an emphasis on reduction of waste and the ability to respond to changes in demand competently and flexibly.

Everything in our scrum approach accelerates the cadence for completion. We see more frequent and expeditious team meetings. We see many more reviews that help to reduce the risk inherent in project activities. We see daily reporting. We see work breakdown structures decomposed down to a level rarely seen in other venues. Instead of waltzing, we are doing a polka—we are in double-time mode.

1.3 Eliminate Waste and Save Money

Scrum focuses not so much on processes and long-term planning and much more so on execution of the short-term plan and identification and prompt removal of obstacles. We see no reason to execute futile multitasking exercises that result in non-completion of essential work breakdown elements. We have been disappointed too many times by project managers who think they can schedule tight projects with an unrealistic critical path and expect their team to overcome wishful thinking by brute force. Our scrum approach eliminates prescience for all but the nearest sprint period, be that two weeks or thirty days. Because of the numerous in-process reviews, managers remain completely aware of task status, failures to complete, and any drift toward the multitasking delusion.

The reduced cycle time saves money due to the decrease in risk and the focused completion of work breakdown elements. Because we spend less time on nonessential elements, we also eliminate some process waste, especially the waste caused by context-switching during multitasking.

1.4 Product Requirements

The scrum approach advocates intensified participation by the customer in much more than the voice of customer phase of the project. This cooperation can reduce some of the dependency on detailed product specifications, although detailed documents remain desirable. If the customer is one who does not wish to participate to the degree required during the project or is unable to do so, then we can anticipate some repercussions on subsequent deliveries. Conventional software or product development is wholly specification-driven. The requirements in those specifications are bound by attributes that constitute good requirements:

1. Traceable
2. Cohesive
3. Complete
4. Consistent

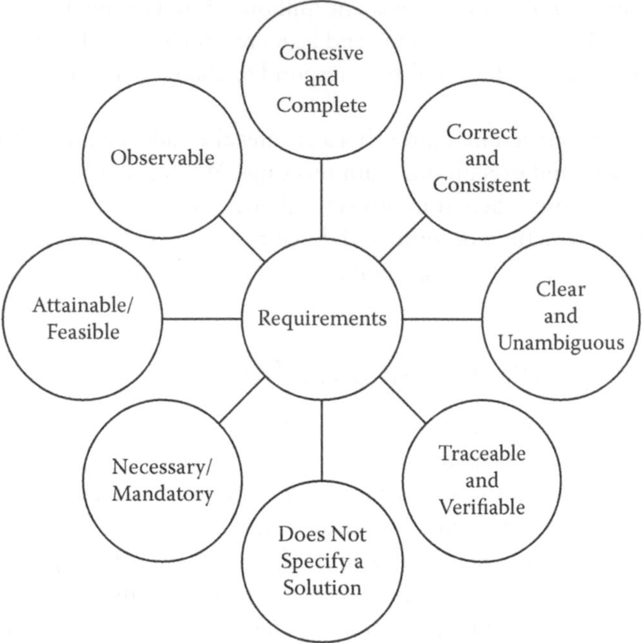

Figure 1.4 Product requirements.

5. Correct
6. Current
7. Externally observable
8. Unambiguous
9. Mandatory
10. Verifiable

With the scrum approach, these constraints are less a concern (although they never disappear from consideration) because the customer has a high degree of interaction and integration with the development team. We see increased verbal exchanges and clarifications occurring, followed by completed, comprehensive, and lean documentation that is used to guide the creation of the product.

Additionally, scrum projects address the product requirements through all design cycles and constant customer interactions to drive the prototypes and product when specific requirements are not known (see Figure 1.4). Whatever the endeavor, the objective—which drives the requirements—must be known and demonstrated or otherwise articulated to the developing organization. In scrum, we deliberately execute our actions using high-frequency meeting cycles, delivering the highest level of system functionality to the customer for review or feedback on the next level of product details.

1.5 Improved Control/Assurance

Improved quality control comes from the communication exchanges and the focus of the team on the immediate product deliverables. One way we can meet the goal of a high-quality, cost-effective product occurs when we integrate the customer as a member of the scrum team.

1.5.1 Lincoln

The power of direction setting and constant monitoring cannot be over-estimated. In the 1860s there were no computers. There were no project tracking tools and Gantt charts. Even the communications were difficult—nothing like telephones and e-mails we have today. Yet President Lincoln managed to keep the project together. In his book, *Lincoln on Leadership*, Donald Phillips describes how Lincoln made use of setting goals and then constantly monitoring the progress and consulting with those responsible for delivering the results.

> As an executive leader, he (Lincoln) channeled this intensity toward the personal goal of preserving the United States as a whole. And it was *progress* toward that goal that Lincoln demanded most, not only of himself, but of those who reported to him.
>
> Establishing goals and gaining their acceptance from subordinates is crucial for effective leadership. Goals unify people, motivate them, focus their talent and energy. Lincoln united his followers with the "corporate mission" of preserving the Union and abolishing slavery, and this objective became more firm and resolute with the onslaught of civil war. Even so, Lincoln realized that the attainment of a successful outcome had to be accomplished in steps. So he constantly set specific short-term goals that his generals and cabinet members could focus on with intent and immediacy.[6]

Lincoln knew that setting the direction that his people could support was the only way to be successful. He set short-term objectives and targets and then made sure that they worked diligently to meet these objectives. This is much the theme within the scrum approach. Donald Phillips's book also illustrates that he was adept at handling conflicts.

> Lincoln did not shun conflict. Instead he resolved dissension among his subordinates in a timely manner, knowing full well that it could serve only to further delay progress. Lincoln realized, as do most leaders, that roadblocks and unresolved conflicts simply gum up the works and slow achievement. And he frequently preached this concept to his subordinates . . . . Lincoln created a contagious enthusiasm among followers by demonstrating a sense of urgency toward the attainment of his goal.[7]

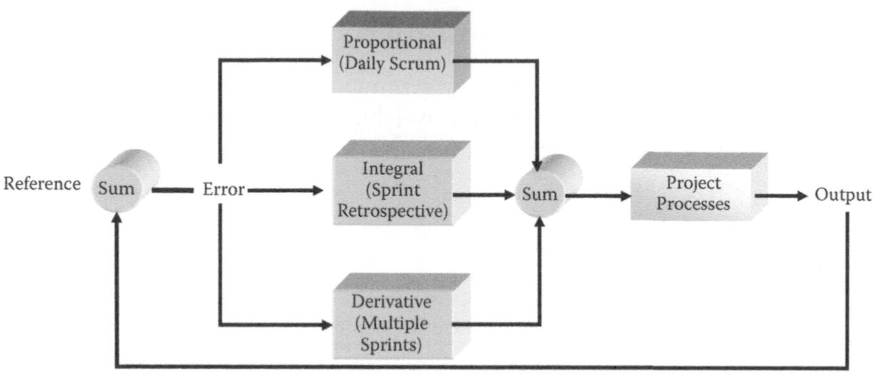

Figure 1.5 Scrum as a control system.

So, what does this mean to the scrum approach? It means that about 150 years ago, thoughtful people knew the importance of setting clear objectives and *constant* monitoring for results and clearing away obstacles. Setting quick, short-term goals and following up and removing obstacles that prevented achieving the objectives was important then and is even more so in today's world of constant distraction.

If we make a control system analogy, we sample the output to provide feedback on current system performance, which we compare to the desired performance and then we make necessary adjustments *to bring the system back to the desired value or course.* The speedier the sampling frequency, the more prompt the possible response from the system and the less the deviation from the desired result. In other words, we can't expect the system to respond more quickly than the speediest sampling rate. We differentiate between a critically damped system and an under-damped system or from the perfect response rate and one that allows for wild fluctuations (see Figure 1.5).

In addition to the sampling impacts, the actual variable sampled and the algorithm for manipulation of the incoming information is important. What do the incoming samples, turned into information, tell us about the state of the system? Figure 1.6 shows the effect of frequent course corrections. Clearly, the more time we lose waiting to make a course correction, the larger the correction is likely to be.

Customer involvement makes it possible to answer questions during development rather than making assumptions about the product based solely on potentially ambiguous specifications. We can argue that no matter the project methodology used, constant confirmation of product designs with customers is good practice.

1.6 Schedule Maintenance

The scrum approach is the essence of simplicity. We define the short-range schedule for a very short duration, say, a semi-month (slightly more than two weeks) to a full month or, in some cases, two-week increments. We derive the items on this

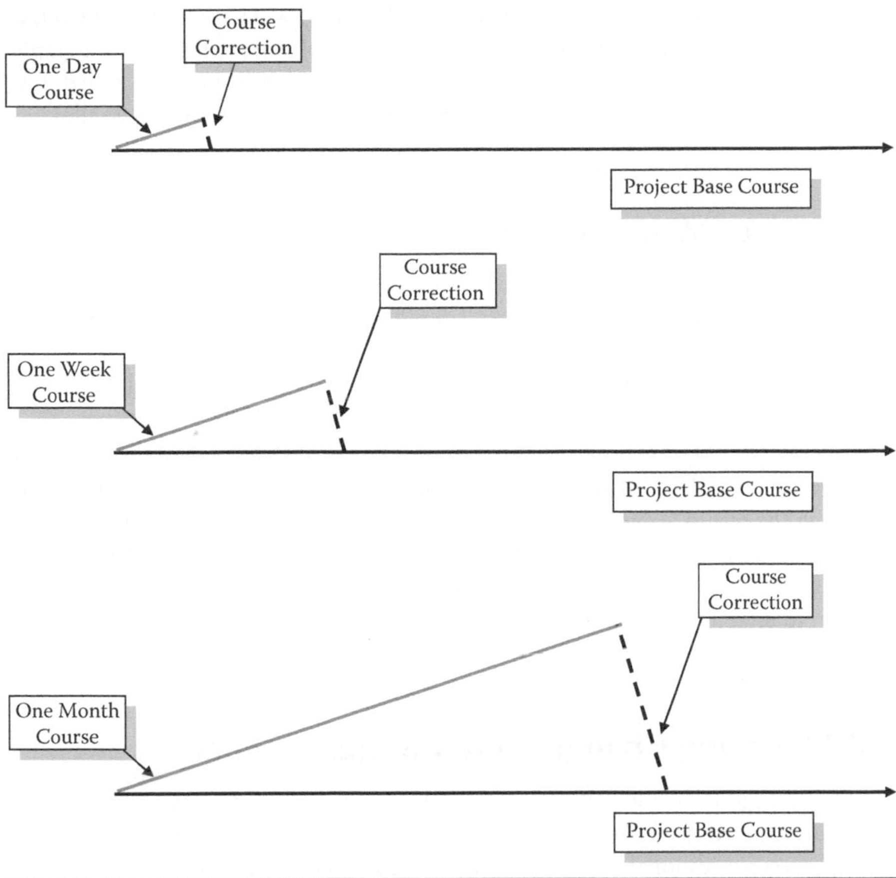

Figure 1.6 Scrum project control.

short-range schedule—the sprint backlog—from a much larger list of activities called the product backlog. Frequent short reviews are sometimes called in-process reviews, a term derived from Department of Defense usage. In the book, *Agile Estimating and Planning*, Mike Cohn identifies levels of planning and subsequent schedule creation, which can be broken down into the following data structure:[8]

1. Day
2. Iteration
3. Release
4. Product
5. Portfolio
6. Strategy

Often, project managers build complex, improperly connected project schedules using a tool like Microsoft Project. The planning horizon might be eighteen months to three years. Assuming they baseline their schedule, they will have to enter the actual time and budget results as the project progresses. The software will generate a graphical image of the separation between plan and reality. In the short-term scheduling approach, this gap between reality and plan will be shortened if it exists at all.

1.7 Budget Maintenance

Budget maintenance fits into a similar control analogy as the communication plan and the schedule. Quick and recurring sample points allow for rapid comparisons to the baseline with the possibility of responding appropriately to the interpretation of those results. The sampling time and the system response time greatly affect the overall liveliness of the system.

In order for budget maintenance to be timely, the finance portion of the enterprise must be capable of generating reports in the same frequency with which we are executing the scrum approach: daily for the scrum meetings and, with more detail, biweekly for the sprint meetings. We expect to see a separation between capital expenditures and noncapital expenses. We will be comparing actual expenses versus the plan to establish the budget gap.

1.8 Managing Changing User Requirements

Product change is an inevitable aspect of the development process. As the product comes to fruition, the customers and their end-users may decide that the product needs additional features. Moreover, some changes to requirements may occur due to interpretations (and misinterpretations) of the existing design or product requirements. Further, change happens as opportunities arise for which customers believe they can take advantage. Customers are unlikely to forgive rigid suppliers.

> The emphasis you agree on now is likely to change over time, perhaps in response to a change in customer needs or as a result of one segment performing significantly better or worse than expected. Customers are also unlikely to remain in the same group forever, so make sure that you and your team watch for this and respond flexibly and quickly.[9]

The point we are making is that we want to use any approach that allows us to flex with our customers and also provides for group learning as the project or task progresses.

Some tactics of project managers ignore acknowledgment of change—it simply can't be allowed during the development work (the "ostrich" approach). Some projects have tight controls over changes to the product (this is a good idea no matter the development philosophy). Rampant, uncontrolled change will never help deliver the product on time. Practitioners of the scrum approach acknowledge and accept that changes occur, providing a mechanism for controlling the impact of changes. If we view customer changes from our agile philosophy, we can see that customer changes are a profit-making opportunity and our scrum approach allows us to make these changes with much lower risk. Of course, we should still re-quote the cost of the project and recalibrate the schedule.

1.9 Are All Projects Candidates for Scrum?

Large-scale scrum is called "scrum of scrums." The idea is to cascade the scrum task lists in a strictly hierarchical manner such that we have assigned all tasks at a given level. We don't see much value in going beyond two levels; however, technological changes may make it easier to manage a multilevel cascade of scrum teams. Conceptually, we see no difficulty with more than two levels; however, in practice, we need to have the means to communicate up and down the hierarchy as well as manage all the schedule and budget activities (see Figure 1.7).

The trick to managing cascading tasks lies in the built-in hierarchy of these items. Neither spreadsheet nor databases lend themselves to cascading, although spreadsheets have the ability to hypertext. One possible alternative would be to use a tree tool like Mindjet's Mind Manager mind-mapping tool and begin with a hierarchical approach from the commencement of the project.

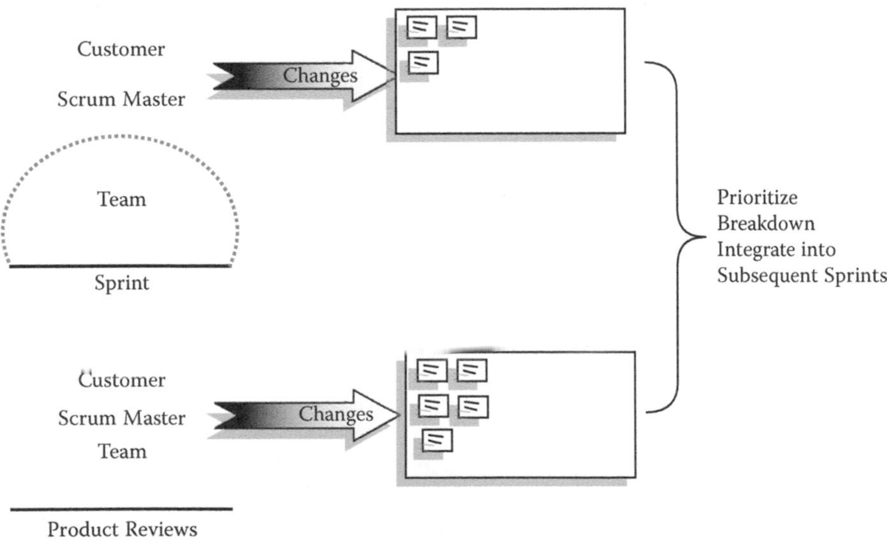

Figure 1.7 Change management.

We have seen the use of cascading strategies and measurement schemes with Balanced Scorecard approach. Kaplan and Norton show how they would use this approach, including strategy maps in addition to the scorecards. Our bottom line is to use the most effective tool for the complexity of the task at hand.

Notes

1. Kimball Fisher, *Leading Self-Directed Work Teams*, (New York, NY: McGraw-Hill, 1993), 32.
2. Kent Beck, et al., *Manifesto for Agile Software Development*, (February 2001), `http://agilemanifesto.org/` (accessed June 20, 2009).
3. Tom Poppendieck, *The Agile Customer's Toolkit*, (2003), `http://www.poppendieck.com/pdfs/AgileCustomersToolkitPaper.pdf` (accessed June 16, 2009).
4. George Stepanek, *Software Project Secrets, Why Software Projects Fail*, (New York, NY: APRESS, 2005), 8.
5. Geoffrey M. Bellman, *Getting Things Done, When You Are Not In Charge*, (San Francisco, CA: Barrett-Koehler Publishers Inc., 2001), 23.
6. Donald T. Phillips, *Lincoln on Leadership*, (New York, NY: Warner Books, Inc., 1992), 109–110.
7. Donald T. Phillips, *Lincoln on Leadership*, (New York, NY: Warner Books, Inc., 1992), 110–111.
8. Mike Cohn, *Agile Estimating and Planning*, (Upper Saddle River, NJ: Prentice Hall Professional Technical Reference, 2006).
9. Andy Bruce and Ken Langdon, *Putting Customers First*, (New York, NY: DK Press, 2002), 19.

Chapter 2

Scrum Basics

2.1 Overview of Scrum

In traditional product development, we decompose the project into a set of phases and execute previously dictated tasks within each phase. This approach is sometimes called the "staged-gate" approach. The conceptual discussion starts with the customer demand or need that must be met. Upon identification of the customer needs, the development moves through the various product launch process phases until arriving at the final testing process, after which the product is released to production and subsequently delivered to the customer.

While using an extreme waterfall model (no overlapping), each of these phases comes to completion before starting the next phase. In actuality, such lack of phase overlapping is seldom the case on real projects although there is no rule for how often to update specifications, products, and verification activities. Figure 2.1 shows a high-level picture of a generic launch process. Enterprises may break these four phases down into many more "gates;" for example, some launch processes at Ford Motor Company have as many as twelve gates.

Product development using the scrum approach always includes periodic activities such as the daily scrum meeting and the sprint meetings. We expect multiple outputs from the project team, incrementally improving the product with time. At each increment, we test and then deliver the product to the customer to *exercise*, allowing for customer feedback.

A principle of scrum is that frequent repetition allows for changes that arise during product development. Instead of trying to contain change, scrum and agile development processes in general propose that the product adapt to the demands of customers over time.

Using conventional project management techniques, the project manager, sometimes with the collusion of the project team, creates a project plan that may span

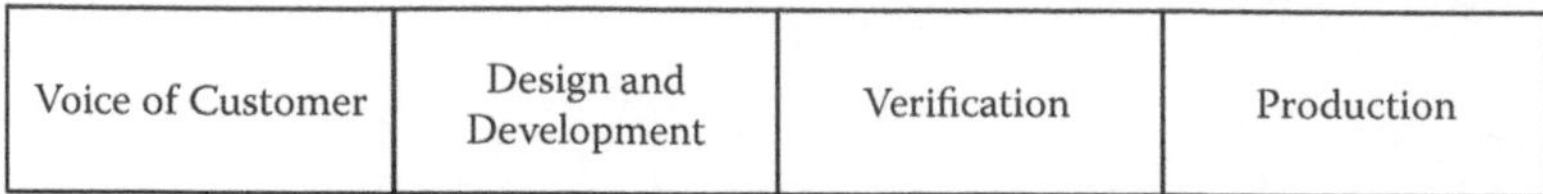

Figure 2.1 Overview of product development.

from several months up to a number of years. While the scrum approach avoids prognostication, project plans are not forbidden.

The scrum approach can work within the boundaries of the project plan. However, from a scrum aspect, the typical useful planning horizon occurs over weeks not years, and the scheduled activities are explicit and attainable.

We inaugurate any project by identifying deliverable items—these are roughly equivalent to the scope of the project and amount to the supposed *voice of the customer*. During this phase, we generate specific functions and performance expectations which will eventually become the product backlog. Customer inputs and the special list, we call the product backlog, go hand-in-hand (see Figure 2.2).

2.2 Requirements

We can gather product intelligence using a variety of ways. Listed below are frequently used methods for gaining an understanding of customer needs. These methods are not exclusive to scrum implementation. We use these activities when we want to research customer demands related to our project.

- Product walk throughs
- Role modeling
- Customer interviews
- Surveys
- Observations of potential customers (ethnography)

With any product development project—including scrum projects—ideas for the content of the product originate most commonly with the customer, although the developer may add some innovations also. We should manage the addition of innovations carefully so that we can avoid "gold-plating" the product design by adding undesirable and, occasionally, dangerous product features. Since scrum increases review frequency from every few months to every few weeks and every day, the risk from changes will be diminished or eliminated.

2.2.1 Use Cases

Requirements capture is part of all developing projects and thus we find it used with scrum and agile development. One standardized approach is to create use cases, a technique defined by the Object Management Group (OMG) in several Unified

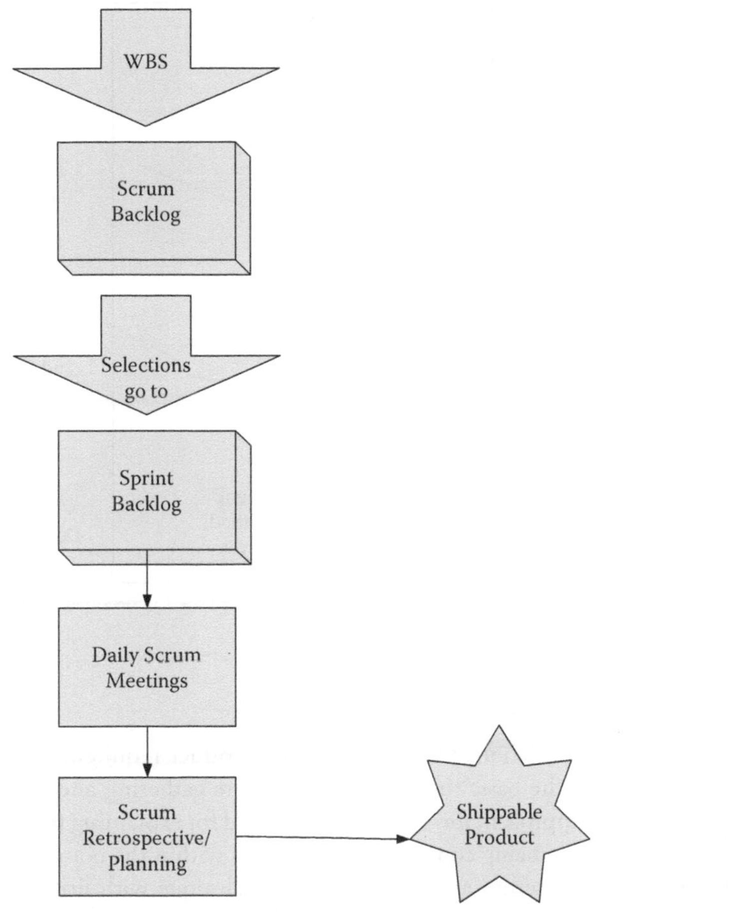

Figure 2.2 Overview of scrum project.

Modeling Language (UML) specifications over the last decade and a half. The simple-to-understand graphical and textual approach streamlines functional requirements capture and improves the interaction of customers with product development. This approach cuts superfluous information from the specification and shortens the time to deliver these requirements to development. We also note that the use case technique is amenable to the use of template documents. The use case method meets the minimum documentation needs of scrum and agile methodologies.

Use cases make significant use of graphics to illustrate how the customer will use the product; use cases accomplish their goal by displaying interactions among users, which typically consist of a number of scenarios that show specific end-user interactions with the product and the response of the product to those interactions (see Figure 2.3).

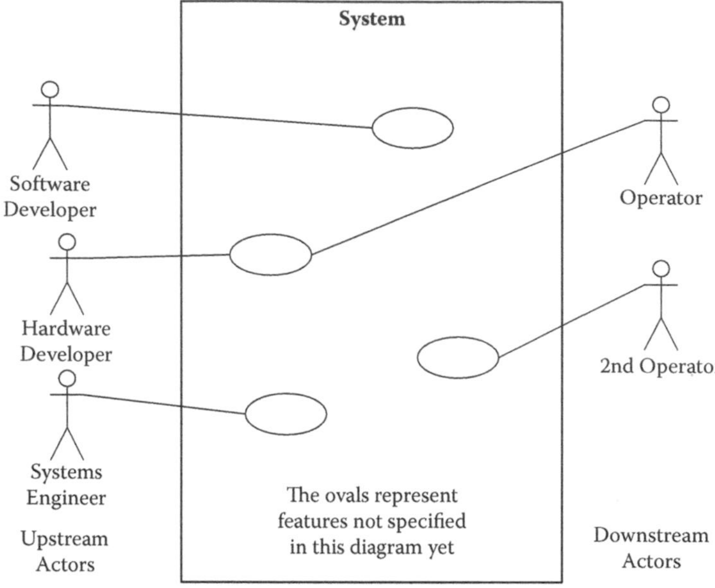

Figure 2.3 Example of use case.

2.2.2 User Stories

There are many variations when it comes to product requirements. For now, we will elaborate on the basic theme of requirements gathering and recording. When using the scrum approach, *user stories* are a method for explaining requirements. User stories benefit from being concise, often dwelling within the boundaries of an index card. Since we use scrum as a high-intensity technique with little waste, extensive and redundant documentation is undesirable. Sometimes, by the time we record or derive all of the requirements, some of the requirements have already metamorphosed into something else or disappeared, requiring revision of the specification. If the development process is cyclic, then each release of the product received by the customer will likely generate even more change requests, requiring even more documentation; in a heavy-handed documentation process, the development process itself can get bogged down in paper generation.

For scrum, the requirements are captured on sticky notes or on index cards. The user story itself is concise and written from the perspective of customer interaction with the product. These cards are place holders for the features that are to be delivered. Interactions, some of which are reviews, with the customer produce the details that the developers capture on these cards. The user story goes somewhat beyond the use case in putting an end-user "face" on the behavior of the feature.

There is no substitute for discussions with the customer when it comes to understanding the target product. This behavior is especially valid when considering the amount of time it takes to develop heavy-handed requirements documents.

The customer will be able to get historical fuel economy information from the vehicle

Figure 2.4 Sprint objectives.

To increase effectiveness, the customer can participate in writing the user stories since they should have the domain-specific knowledge required to identify these functions. The developers will not typically have the same level domain knowledge since they are primarily concerned with the implementation of the specification be it in the form of use cases, user stories, or both. Obviously, a holistic approach that involves both developers and customer and, perhaps, end-users can often enhance the probability of delivering a salable product. We might ask ourselves:

- How many different varieties of customers will use this product?
- What are the product requirements needed to fulfill these customer needs?
- How will diverse customers use the product?

For scrum, it is more important to know the business needs of the software or hardware than to have complicated technical documentation of the product. It is more important to get the user story and how the product will be used in the context of the customer. Additionally, scrum places a high value on customer interaction and not all in the form of formal documentation. It is best when the customer writes the user story. The user story may generate questions that are handled directly with the customer to allow the developer to really understand the goal or objective of the user story through this customer interaction (see Figure 2.4). We would like to emphasize that the scrum approach is not document-averse but, rather, seeks a leaner solution to formulating the requirements for the product.

In our proto-scrum example, documentation was generated just prior to the features introduction. This documentation was not as streamlined as we would expect with scrum; however, neither was it the complicated and heavy-handed technical documentation that is typically associated with waterfall development and other crystalline launch models.

2.2.3 Story Board

The story board tracks the user stories through the various stages of the development process. Typically, this is a white board with all of the sticky notes or index cards of the requirements arrayed on it in some sensible arrangement. The white board is

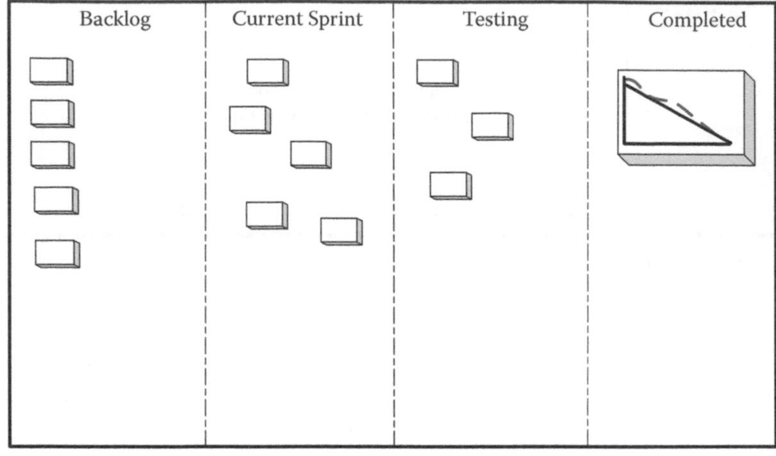

Figure 2.5 Story board.

divided up into sections in order to represent the delivery process. Using an affinity diagram approach during the early phases of concept development is an option. Affinity diagrams occur when we cluster our notes or cards by general theme. The affinity diagram approach would probably not make any sense as we proceed out of concept development.

While the structure and content have some variation, the basics are illustrated in Figure 2.5. In our example, the overall status is tracked as well as the backlog, sprint, and testing status. The various project statuses are posted on a white board or dry erase board with the sticky notes or cards attached directly. The documented deliverables are readily moveable, lending flexibility to the process. The requirements physically move through the project and on this project board. Additionally, this project board provides a clear view of the accomplishments as well as a glimpse of the future deliveries. In essence, the story board provides a key component found in lean implementations in manufacturing facilities; to whit, the visual system.

All of this information on project status is visible, instead of looking up the latest revision of a work order, project document, or excel spreadsheet. The team is responsible for maintaining the story board, which provides increased participation by the people who will be doing the work.

2.2.4 The Spike

While not really a scrum attribute—the "spike" is an agile process that applies to the scrum. In situations where the time to implement a technical solution is not readily known, the user story is broken up into two parts. The spike, the first part, is the investigation to acquire enough knowledge to be able to estimate the work to produce the user story.

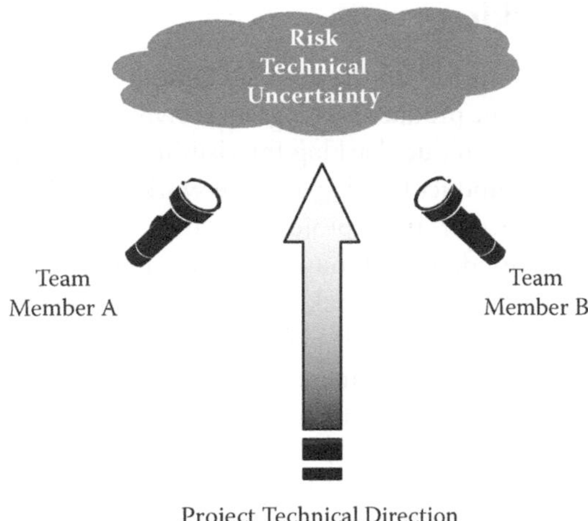

Figure 2.6 Spike objectives.

The intent of the spike is to clarify the risk due to technical uncertainty within the project. Two players from the scrum team will investigate the technology to become more familiar with what will be required to be successful using this new technology within the project (see Figure 2.6). The second part of the spike is the post-research, execution phase of the story implementation.

2.2.5 Lack of Customer Participation

Since practitioners of the scrum approach tend to set priorities using customer feedback rather than rigid, formalized, long lead-time documentation, the customer should be part of the discussion. We can ask the customer or end-users to participate in all of the impedimenta of project development:

- Project reviews
- Product reviews
- Process reviews
- Sprint reviews (scrum-based activity)
- Product backlog reviews (scrum-based activity)
- Daily scrum reviews (not as likely as the previous items)

Regardless of the documentation workload, reviews are generally a good practice since they provide motivation for interparty communications. If we implement the scrum approach, we may see some balking by the customer due to the frequency of the reviews; hence, we should use good judgment when making our invitations to reviews.

2.3 Product Backlog

The product backlog is a list of all the tasks we intend to do during a substantial duration; for example, some product backlogs may involve multiyear projects. Every task must be listed in the product backlog for visibility to the team. We will show later on how we tie the product backlog and the work breakdown structure (work breakdown structure) together. If the project, product, or process merits a large list, we might expect to see hundreds or thousands of line items.

We set priorities for the product backlog based on the customer's and technical needs (see Figure 2.7). The product backlog can include relevant documentation for the upcoming sprints. The documentation can be generated as the precursor for subsequent sprints. Each successive sprint produces additional design details, functionality, and verification activities.

Both the product and the sprint backlogs provide opportunities for the use of "kanban." Kanban effectively signals that something is ready for work. We often see the use of kanban in lean manufacturing environments, but kanban are not restricted to manufacturing. The idea of kanban is to use them as part of a pull system rather than a push system. In a push system, the manager or Scrum Master might issue work orders based on some system for doing so. In a pull system, the scrum team members will select the components for work (see Figure 2.8). We will describe the process more fully in Section 2.6.2, "Sprint Backlog."

2.4 Planning and Estimation

Estimations, part of the planning activities of the project, are always guesses, which can vary wildly in quality, sometimes without much thought going into which actions are needed to produce the deliverable. This limitation is overcome with some forethought and dissection of the deliverable into its constituent tasks.

One source of planning failures, the long time horizon, occurs when planning is too far out to predict reasonably accurately. Planning failures can happen anywhere where a long-term estimation is required—the problem can be reduced partially by acknowledging the variation in estimate tolerances as the project progresses from concept phases through the actual development work and delivery. Some duration estimation techniques (for example, Program Evaluation and Review Technique [PERT]) attempt to identify the risks inherent in long-range estimations and provide a contingency plan for mitigating, managing, or eliminating the risk.

The project manager can use a variety of project duration estimation methodologies (for example, PERT or critical path approaches). Technical duration estimations are necessary in all projects. Since projects are, by definition, unique, historical data may not provide the information we really need in order to provide reasonable estimations. If historical data is available, we recommend visiting this source of information and mining it for data, particularly any information regarding scheduling anomalies and complete delivery and budget failures.

ITEM	DESCRIPTION	DAYS	RESPONSIBLE	PRIORITY	Advance	Comments
1	Medium instrumentation new test equipment		Al		75%	Waitiing for fixture
2	Module 1 functional tester	15	Al		60%	
3	Small cluster line sequencing implementation		Gus		85%	
4	Large instrumentation ICONS verification with external light		Gus		50%	
5	Gauges calibrator	15	Mano		90%	
6	Release firmware docs with new format to implement serialization	7	Mano		75%	
7	Transferring old programmer info to the new one	4	Mano		50%	
8	Write software for the gauges calibration and tester for EastCust.	15	Mano		90%	
9	Quote pin detector for instrumentation	5	John		20%	
10	Implement 2010 program	7	John		90%	
11	Modify rotary test program to test units without marking them on demand	1	John		95%	
12	Implement serialization for line haul	7	John		90%	
13	Carolina UREA in-circuit tester quote	4	Evan		50%	

Figure 2.7 Example of product backlog.

ITEM	*DESCRIPTION*	*DAYS*	*RESPONSIBLE*	*PRIORITY*	*Advance*	*Comments*
14	Modify in-circuit tester program to test for printed circuit board A1B	1	Evan		80%	
15	Moduel 1 in-circuit testing implementation	1	Evan		0%	
16	Auxiliary gauge in-circuit testing modification	3	Evan		0%	
17	Quote area 2' & 5'	4	Evan		0%	
18	Modify part numbers 4, 5, and 6	1	Evan		66%	
19	Make changes on severe environment instrumentation according to spec	1	Evan		50%	
20	Modify cherry picker electronic device	3	Robert		85%	
21	Heavy instrument new versions implementation	3	Robert		60%	
22	Develop spare parts database FF2	10	Sergei		10%	
23	Install interface to use only one computer and terminals for visual aids	5	Paul		10%	
24	Implement NextGen program	7	Paul		95%	

Figure 2.7 Example of product backlog. (*Continued*)

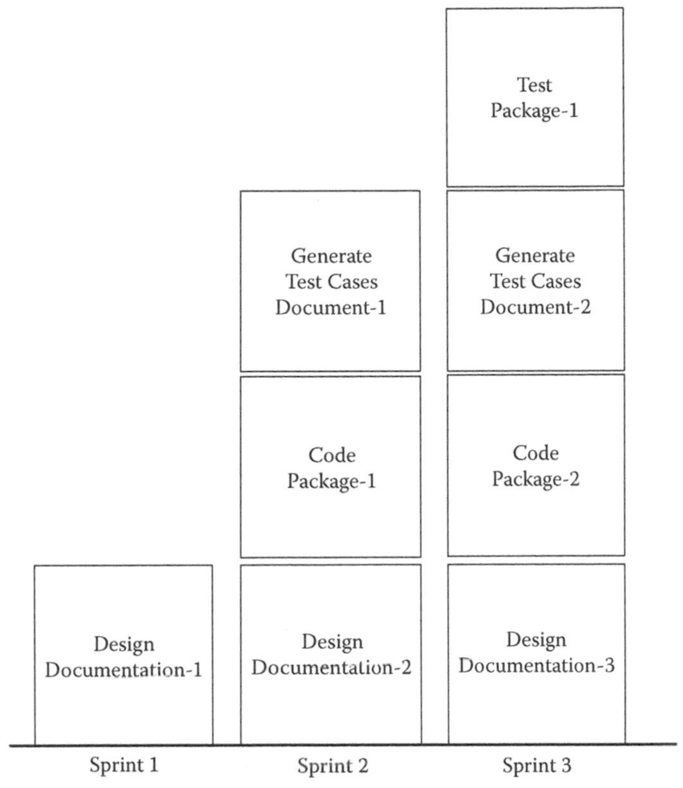

Figure 2.8 Example of sprint objectives.

2.4.1 Historical Information

Using any historical method, the organization will make use of its experience with numerous projects, individuals, and teams. It is possible to reduce the level of uncertainty by knowing the past performance (assuming that past performance is a predictor of future performance). This kind of information is sometimes called "tribal knowledge" or "lore." For example, one of us, as the manager of an electrical/electronics verification group, knows that when getting a vehicle for systems integration testing, it will generally take one week to turn a vehicle from its typical delivered level of functionality to the level suitable for systems integration testing. This is fairly repeatable and is helpful when it comes to planning.

Historical information has limitations when it comes to *new* activities. There is no historical information available when working with a new supplier or new technology. However, it may be possible to mitigate some of the risk by comparing the new situation to some historical aspect.

2.4.2 Subject Matter Experts

If the organization has people with experience in the area requiring estimation, we may define these individuals to be subject matter experts. In some cases, it may make sense to elicit estimates from more than one subject matter expert using a tool like planning poker. The differences between or among the estimates can offer a glimpse into the uncertainty underlying budget and schedule estimates. As we have indicated, we consider it prudent to avoid any action that would drive the team toward groupthink.

2.4.3 PERT

As with conventional projects, the use of PERT can help with estimation for task durations. PERT attempts to address the range of possible dates for tasks that are especially risky. We do this by averaging the range of possible durations, in this case, slightly weighted toward the *most probable*. We can use a spreadsheet program to make this approach easy to use as well as provide instantaneous estimates.

While some elements of a project may recur from project to project, such as a well-defined software release process, many elements occur as "one-off" activities. The project manager can use recurrent elements to enhance the accuracy of the forecast due to the reduced uncertainty of the estimates. Asserting the duration of a nonrecurrent task as a single value implies extensive foreknowledge. Describing the task duration as a range of possibilities reflects the uncertainty of project execution. PERT uses a network analysis based on events defined within the project and addresses one-off durations; it allows the project team to express durations as a span of likelihoods. The U.S. Department of Defense classifies estimates as pessimistic, optimistic, and probable. The team weighs its classifications with the heaviest weight going to the most probable scenario. The PERT equation appears as follows:

$$Duration = [(Pessimistic + 4 \times Most\ probable + Optimistic)/6]$$

Note that the formula hints at a potentially unjustified normal distribution around the most probable scenario.

PERT provides a framework for simulation. A software tool (@Risk®) exists that provides simulation capability to Microsoft Project®.

The PERT estimation technique also provides the project manager with a glimpse of the uncertainty of the estimates. However, the range of values (Pessimistic–Optimistic) provides a strong indicator of the certainty used by the estimator. The project manager will convert this value into the task variance using the equation below. The larger the task variance, the more uncertain the estimate:

$$Task\ Variance = [(Pessimistic - Optimistic)/6]2$$

Variations in the three PERT estimates implies uncertainty. However, if the project manager assumes the estimate of time follows a normal distribution, then he

Table 2.1 Sigma and Probability

1 sigma	68.26%
2 sigma	95.46%
3 sigma	99.73%
6 sigma	99.99+%

Source: Pries, K. and Quigley, J. *Project Management of Complex and Embedded Systems*, Taylor & Francis, Boca Raton, FL., 2008

can refine or broaden the estimates. Taking the individual estimates to the one, two, three, or six standard deviations (sigma or σ) spreads the available time and improves the probability that the estimate lies within the range of dates. See Table 2.1.

Figure 2.9 illustrates the effect of variation.

For a confidence interval of 99.73%, the range of possibilities varies from 3 to 19.7 hours. Estimates with substantial variation should be removed from the critical path or receive risk mitigation. Critical path dates with high variation represent risky goals. PERT models become complicated because the software must iterate through permutations of the three levels—the more tasks/deliverables, the longer it takes for the model to converge.

We can expand on the PERT concept by using Monte Carlo simulation. If we have enough historical data to assess the probability parameters for a probability distribution function (mean and variance for the normal distribution), we can use a random number generator to feed the inverse of the distribution function. The result of this formulation is a simulation of the potential duration or budget value for this activity in the project. We would use our Monte Carlo model on specific and well-known activities. If we are able to use a Monte Carlo model on all tasks in a project, then we can generate an estimate for the project as a whole.

2.4.4 Story Points

Story points are based on a short description of a set of features called user stories, which we discussed earlier. User stories often have the following set of features:

- Feature descriptions from anyone on the team or any customer.
  - Team features are derived.
  - Customer features are usually primary (although an implicit feature can overshadow these; e.g., an operating system in real-time software development).
- Generally use a template to improve consistency of communication.
- Have items that can be seen or tested in the review.
- Are estimated in terms of hours, days, or "story points".
- Are independent from other stories (ideally).

Project Time Estimate												
Doc Reg Number:		Project Responsible	Prepared by:	Page_1_of__			Product Name					
Prj. Responsible:		Key Date	Est Reg Date (Orig) ________ (Rev) ________									
Core Team												
WBS designation	WBS description	Task estimate responsible	Optimistic estimate (hours)	Most likely estimate (hours)	Pessimistic estimate (hours)	Task variance (+/−)	Calc. estimate value (68%)		Calc. estimate value (95%)		Calc. estimate value (99.73%)	
1.1.2.	*review hw content*	*JMQ*	*5*	*12*	*15*	*2.8*	*8.6*	*15.2*	*5.8*	*16.9*	*3.0*	*19.7*
						0.0	*0.0*	*0.0*	*0.0*	*0.0*	*0.0*	*0.0*
						0.0	*0.0*	*0.0*	*0.0*	*0.0*	*0.0*	*0.0*
						0.0	*0.0*	*0.0*	*0.0*	*0.0*	*0.0*	*0.0*
						0.0	*0.0*	*0.0*	*0.0*	*0.0*	*0.0*	*0.0*
						0.0	*0.0*	*0.0*	*0.0*	*0.0*	*0.0*	*0.0*

Figure 2.9 Duration estimation technique. (From Pries, K. and Quigley, J. *Project Management of Complex and Embedded Systems*, Taylor & Francis, Boca Raton, FL., 2008.)

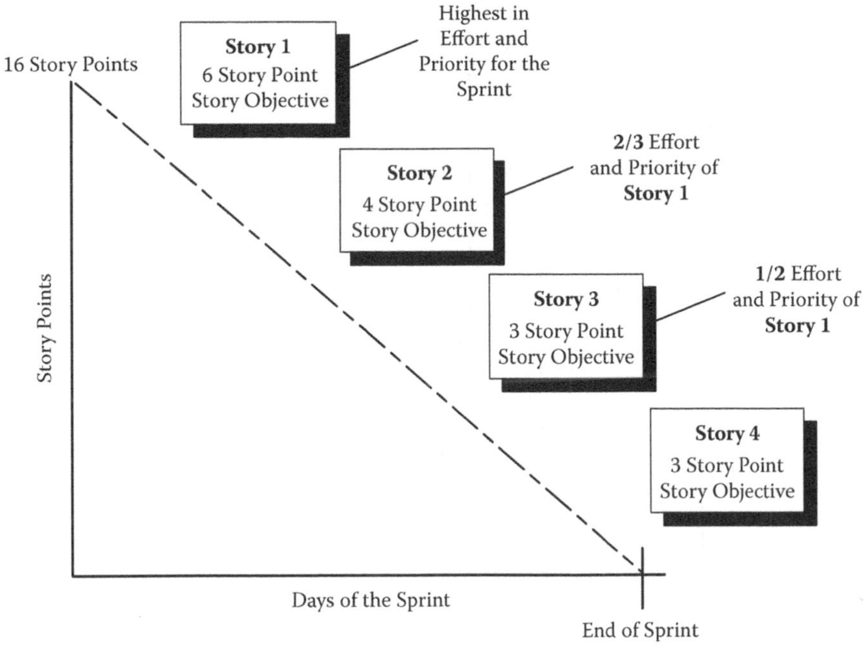

Figure 2.10 Story points.

Story points are a way of estimating the amount of work that we must do. Each "user story" will have a set of story points. In essence, a story point represents an arbitrary unit of measure defined by the team—they are not nearly as formal as software development tools such as function points or feature points. Because they are not formally defined, they can be whatever the team agrees that they are—so long as they help to estimate the durations of tasks. A story point may incorporate multiple days of design, coding, and testing depending on how the team has decided to use this approach. Alternatively, the team may decide to use days or hours.

The team estimates how many story points can be achieved within a sprint. This sets how many of the user stories that have story points can be taken up in a sprint (see Figure 2.10).

2.4.5 Planning Poker

One tool we can use with scrum teams in order to estimate task duration is called planning poker.[1] We will include the entire scrum team in a planning poker exercise. On a scrum project, we will usually see no more than six people. The product owner can participate in planning poker as an auditor or observer (see Figure 2.11).

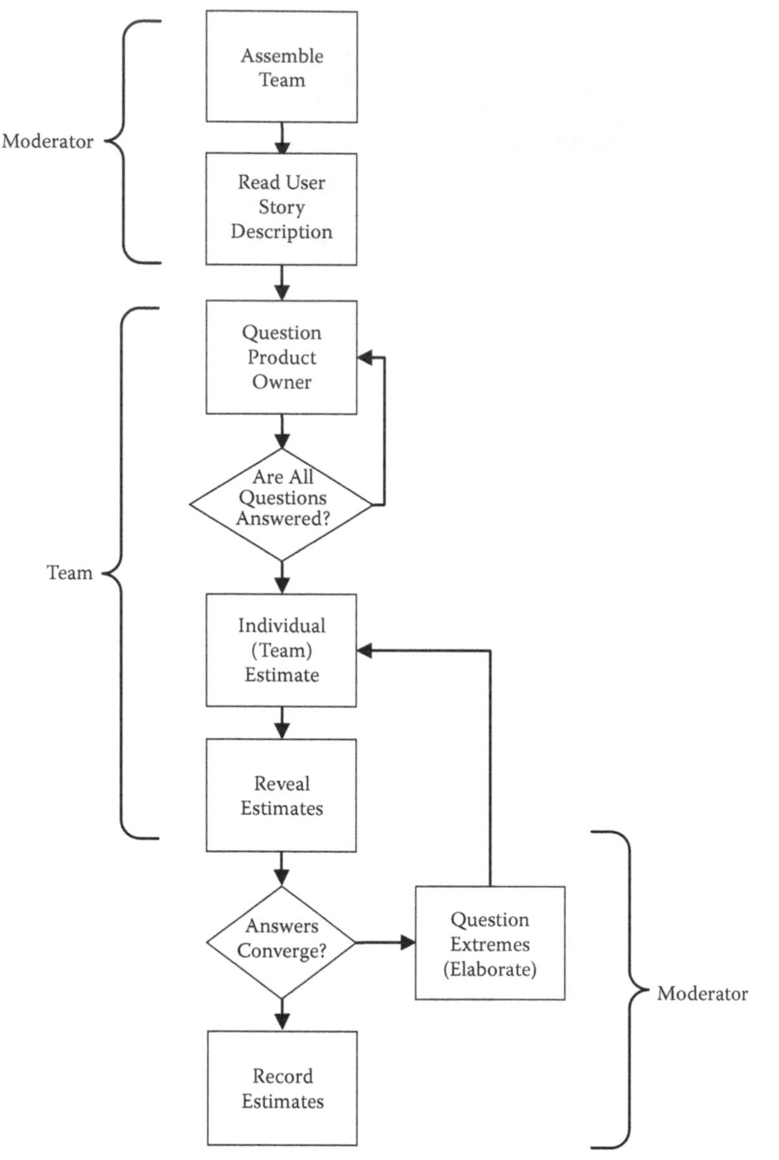

Figure 2.11 Planning poker process.

As we begin the exercise, each team member receives a deck of cards (hence, the name "planning poker"). Each card has written on it one set of valid estimates. We could, for example, use a Fibonacci sequence like 1, 2, 3, 5, 8, 13, 21, 34, 55 or more. The Scrum Master can prepare the cards before the exercise, written in large enough numbers to be easily readable in a small room. We like the idea of reuse, so we can save our cards for the next planning poker exercise.

The Scrum Master orally presents each use case or user story we are trying to estimate. After the Scrum Master answers all questions, each team member confidentially picks a card that has an estimate with which he or she agrees. We do not show the cards until each team member makes a selection. Once all team members have finished their selections, all cards are turned over together and displayed such that all team members view each estimate. When estimates deviate from each other significantly, the high and low team members account for their estimates orally. The idea is to liberate the team member's thinking with respect to the estimate—they may have seen something the rest of the team has not. We need to avoid even the slightest drift toward groupthink during this exercise.

The Scrum Master takes notes throughout the exercise. Once the team discussion subsides or a timer runs out, each member reestimates by drawing a card (draw poker not stud poker!). We repeat the exercise as we related in the previous paragraph. At this point, we often see a confluence of thought about the estimates and the variance decreases. The gist of this approach is not so much accurate/precision but, rather, a sound judgment.

We have used a simple method to encourage dialogue, avoid groupthink, and resolve a collection of informed opinions from a cross section of experts. Also, if the variance does *not decrease* as we go through the exercise, we may have a use case or user story that is so nebulous as to be unusable.

2.5 Release Backlog

The release backlog derives from the product backlog. The release backlog is the list of features intended for each release of the product to the customer. It is a subset of the product backlog and we usually populate it with the highest priority elements demanded by the customer or sometimes we will pick items based on technical dependencies; that is, when the technical issue must be addressed before the customer function can be delivered. The release backlog will be spread over a number of sprints, which is generally determined by the velocity with which the team attains results.

The release backlog can be further broken down into a set of sprint backlogs, with a specific focus for each upcoming sprint. Each backlog incorporates more details from the work breakdown to push toward achieving the objective. The result is that such a sprint will produce a product that will be delivered to the customer for feedback.

2.6 Sprint

The "sprint" is the scrum version of a short-range schedule. The idea is to compile a list of only those activities to which we can commit to complete for the sprint duration (see Figure 2.12). If our approach uses the half-monthly method, we will

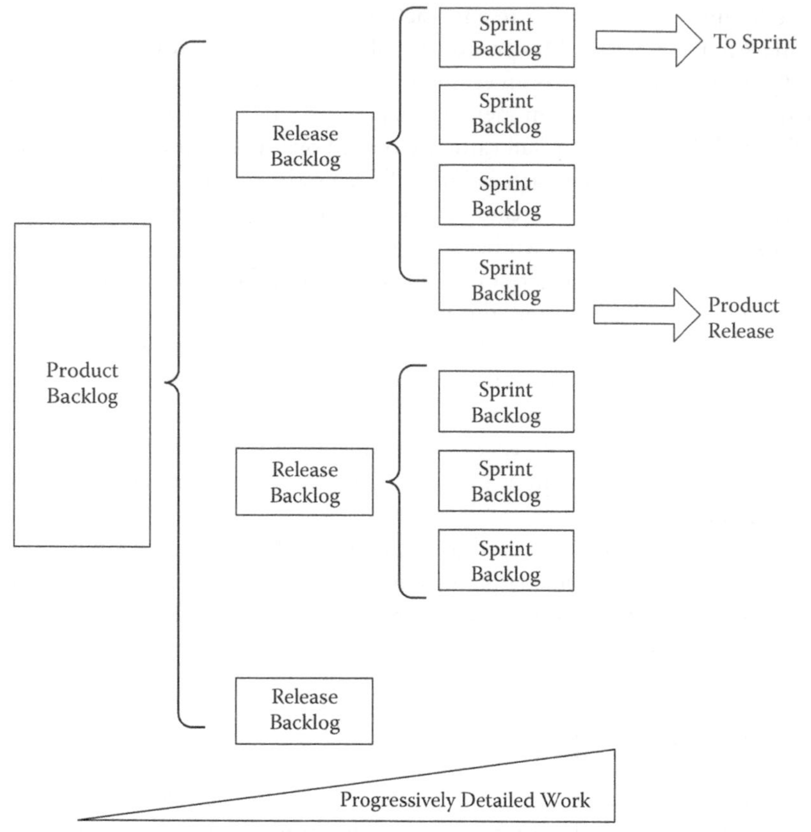

Figure 2.12 Task breakdown.

select a project or parts of projects that we can accomplish within the fourteen-to sixteen-day period of the sprint.

Once we receive approval on a sprint backlog, the list becomes quasi-sacred. Breaking the sprint can only occur when a higher-level manager approves the change based on an extenuating circumstance; in general, we expect the upstream manager to make these changes reluctantly, since the change to the sprint basically breaks the short-range plan. We should always be trying to avoid this kind of outcome because it leads to non-closure on the sprint activities and subsequent delays in product or process release. By demanding commitment to the sprint, we ensure a high level of focus on only those tasks that are listed in the backlog.

We found during actual practice of this high-intensity approach that we had to *discourage* our teams from putting too many activities into the sprint backlog. We indicated the importance of the commitment; furthermore, we made the suggestion that adding items to impress a manager was a misuse of the tool. In situations where we are using the tool for general line management, the team will have a set of routine tasks that do not necessarily fall into the sprint backlog. Hence, it is essential that they avoid the hubris of trying to do too much and failing the sprint.

When compiling a product backlog, the viewpoint of the executor is more important than that of the requestor, which means we accomplish what is attainable instead of making our selections for political reasons or to assuage complaining managers. We also recommend recording the date of submission to the backlog, so we can age files and increase priority. If we do not increase priority with the age of the backlog activity, we can get into a situation where the activity will always be starved by more pressing projects. This type of approach is used with some print queue algorithms for exactly this reason. In print queues (or any other for that matter), it is more efficient to run small jobs before running large jobs. However, the most sophisticated print queue algorithms "age" the large jobs until they finally run.

2.6.1 Sprint Speed

The sprint velocity is the available hours during the defined period of work. This is often referred to as the team's "*velocity.*" The available hours are

$$Sprint\ velocity = People \times hours \times days\ of\ work$$

We account for these hours strictly and compare them against estimates for the tasks and the sprint results. We will critique these accomplishments positively at the end of the sprint. The hours, therefore, must be available hours for work. In short, we are defining real utilization based on actual available hours from the employee and not including time for meals, breaks, and other activities.

The sprint velocity changes as we progress through a project. This is true for all projects, usually with some efficiency losses at the start of the project due to learning curves. These losses at the start are due to

- Unfamiliarity with technology
- Unfamiliarity with the design objectives
- Poor team development (forming, storming, norming, performing)

The Scrum Master can expect the velocity of the team to accelerate as the team proceeds—assuming the team is evolving and we have no major technology issues. Given these constraints, the expected velocity curve over time would look like the curve in Figure 2.13. Additionally, adding people to the sprint has an immediate impact on team throughput as the new player is integrated into the team, becoming familiar with the technology and the scope of the project. Adding people to the project seldom results in an immediate improvement in project throughput. The various scrum meetings facilitate assimilation of new people into the team.

When the activities are measured in story points, the sprint can also be measured in story points.

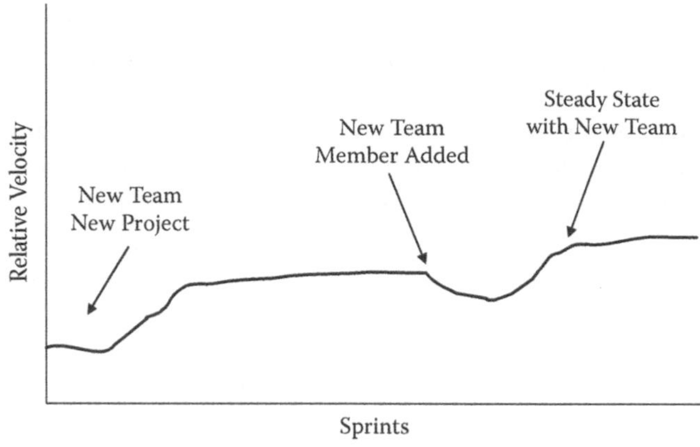

Figure 2.13 Velocity over time and team additions.

2.6.2 Sprint Backlog

The sprint backlog is the table we derive from the product backlog that formalizes the schedule for the sprint (short-range schedule). Note that we don't ignore budget consumption during the sprint, although the focus is largely on getting the tasks completed within the designated duration.

We derive the sprint backlog from the product backlog. The team sets the priorities for the elements in the product backlog and the team identifies the means by which they will achieve the specific product backlog item based on the product backlog priority and the *complete thread*. The *complete thread* is the objective of this particular sprint. A specific product backlog item may take a number of sprint backlog tasks to achieve. It is important to note that these sprint backlog tasks are generated by the team, leading to higher commitment to accomplishment of the sprint goals. Figure 2.14 shows an actual sprint backlog used by a production test equipment department. The percentage of completion shows that the team is working on items that have a realistic chance for completion during the sprint period.

2.6.3 Documentation

Some practitioners think agile development means elimination of documentation. This thinking is erroneous—the methodology espouses minimizing some of the negative consequences of the traditional approach to documentation. The first sprints are often used to document the design requirements and each subsequent sprint adds to the documentation until the entire product is documented. Using this method means documentation is "just in time" for design execution instead of the long months of documentation development, the product of which can often become obsolete by the time the work actually occurs. During the next sprint, while delivering

DESCRIPTION	*StartDate*	*Days*	*Owner*	*PTY*	*Advance*	*Week 31*					*Week 32*					*Week 33*					*Week 34*				
Review BBB traceability matrix	22-Oct-09	5	Alberto	1	50%																				
AAAA Gauges traceability matrix	30-Sep-09	5	Manuel	2	50%																				
Emigrated XYZ from PMSDBA to EPDPROD (edit sation, display and visual aids)	15-Oct-09	5	Manuel	1	75%																				
Rebuild heavy fixture and add to	1-Oct-09	30	Sergio		75%																				
Integrate all hauler products in one equipment	1-Aug-09	5	Raul		50%																				
Change C station to Labview	1-Aug-09	15	Raul	5	50%																				
Led color detector for individual gauges	30-Sep-09	15	Raul	1	50%																				
Develop spare parts database FF2	15-Sep-09	10	Manuel		50%																				
Emigrated AAAA programing station from VB to Labview	15-Sep-09	30	Hector	1	80%																				
Warning light bar traceability matrix	30-Sep-09	5	Hector	3	50%																				
Design programmer for AAAA 2 inches	15-Sep-09	15	Alfredo	3	90%																				
XYZ Calibration tool	30-Sep-09	15	Alfredo	4	90%																				

Figure 2.14 Example of sprint backlog.

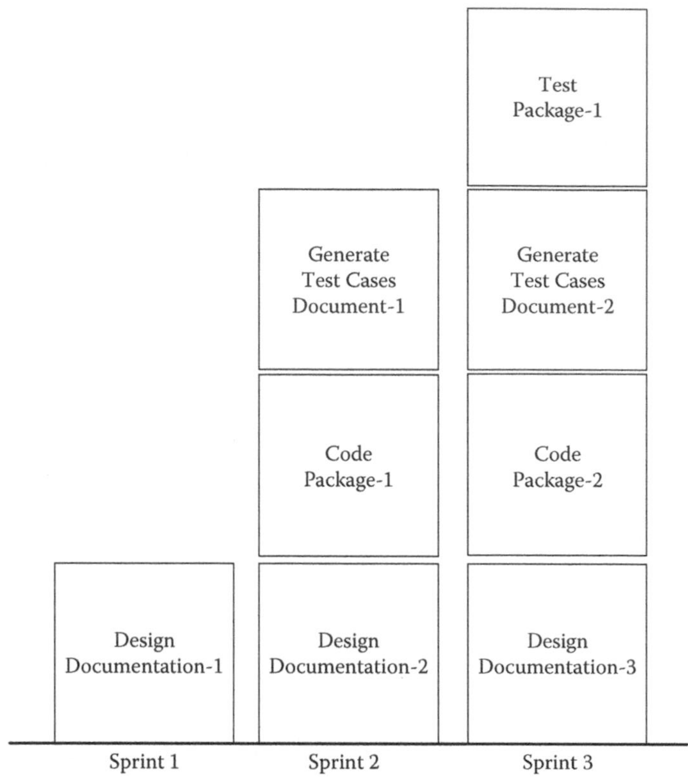

Figure 2.15 Sprint objectives.

to this present revision of documentation, the documentation will increment into the next set of features for the product (see Figure 2.15).

2.6.4 Development

Once we have completed the design documentation during the first sprint, we are now ready for the development work. The software is written or the hardware designed using the direction and details from a product backlog that already has priorities set and form the design documentation. Problems that arise during the development phases are not left to languish but become potential candidates for a sprint backlog. If we are aligning with a traditional staged-gate process, we will set up our sprints so that some of them occur immediately *before* the design gates. That way, we are prepared for the staged-gate with the latest version of the now-reduced product backlog.

We would also like to remember that our goal is to be releasing a sellable product at the end of each sprint. This goal is especially true during development of the product or service, which is often the portion of a project where we have our highest risk.

2.6.5 Verification

The testing staff members are often colocated with the design team. We use the design documentation along with interaction between the development team and the test team to generate the test documentation, which often occurs in parallel with the development effort to meet the previous sprint's design definition. We derive test cases from the design documentation.

This collaboration clarifies the future sprint package of features (product or service) to be delivered to the verification team. Automated test fixtures, software and hardware, are created and updated per the design documentation. The fixtures and test suites are updated as the development documentation is updated and in parallel with the development work. The testing results are quickly communicated back to the developing portion of the team for incorporation as new sprint backlog items. The development team will use these new items to correct defects and integrate the new items into subsequent sprints.

The results of the verification work, the defects found, are tracked within another backlog—the error or fault backlog. Delivering a new version of the product every two weeks to thirty days requires the test team to execute efficiently. In many cases, automation of the test cases is required to match the pace of the development effort and deliveries to the customer.

2.6.5.1 Test before Software

It is not unheard of in agile development to have the test cases developed before the software development activities. When this kind of test development occurs on a function-by-function basis, we call it test-driven design; the defined test will force the appropriate design. Developers that understand how the product will be tested are able to write code or design hardware that will meet the test objectives. In this way, the test cases fulfill the role of the requirements documentation.

One problem with this method is that test defects will propagate into the product much like requirements defects move into the product. Additionally, where no test cases exist, dormant defects remain latent. Exhaustive testing is rarely, if ever, possible, so all details of how the product should work may not be covered. This same problem exists in conventional project management, even when suitable design documentation is available up front. However, in cases where we have design documentation and test documentation, we can construct a traceability matrix to verify that each design requirement has a test or tests that exercise the requirement. Regardless of project management philosophy, traceability matrices provide a simple method for tracking completeness of testing.

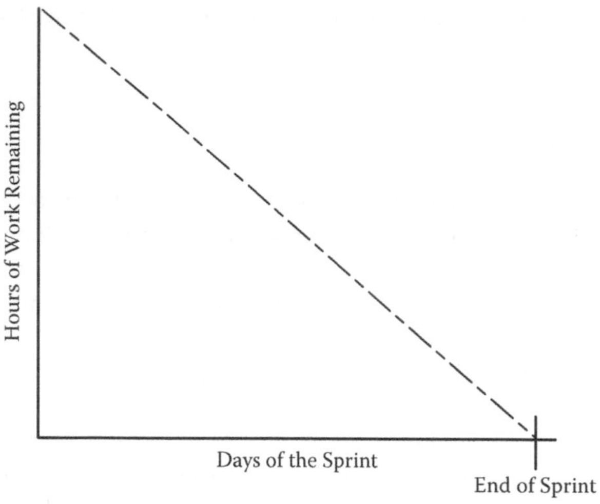

Figure 2.16 Example of ideal burndown chart.

2.6.6 Burndown Chart

The burndown chart is a graphical representation of task completion. Typical burndown charts show accumulated hours to be completed and then measure the actual hours, *consumed* versus the planned hours, to represent consumption of planned hours. The plotted lines will go from high on the left to low on the right. The chart makes it very easy to see if we are on plan.

The rate of productivity, the hours of work accomplished per day, is a key metric to efficiency of the project. Team members can edit the burndown chart directly or provide the information to the Scrum Master for updating on a computer. From the product backlog, we have estimated the amount of work (time) to achieve each of the items included in the backlog. As the team works the backlog items during the sprint, the team (individuals working on each backlog item) documents the amount of time remaining for the tasks within a sprint.

We see no reason not to have a budgetary burndown chart also. In this chart, we would plot actual expenses and capital consumed against budgeted values. The chart makes it readily apparent when the project has excessive spending. Alternatively, capital and expenses could each have their own chart. The decision about how to represent these items is up to the practitioner and will center on the needs of the manager (Scrum Master) and the team.

If the burndown charts are maintained daily, then the manager should have updates to the data that are no more than one day old. In itself, this approach will reduce risk, since the updates occur promptly. Maintaining these charts consumes resources, but we feel the element of control gained from this practice outweighs any potential negatives. Figure 2.16 illustrates an ideal burndown chart.

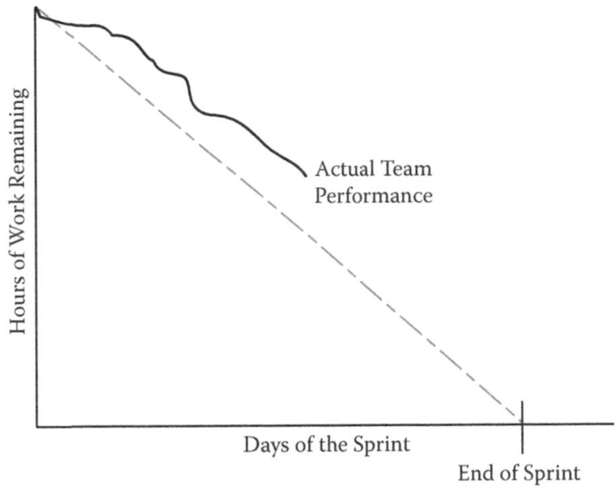

Figure 2.17 Underestimated burndown chart.

As conventional project management approaches, scrum project management is subject to the quality of the estimates for the work to be performed. However, the scrum approach accounts for these estimates better than the typical project management methodology in that it allows for adjustment of the sprint scope during the sprint. In reality, this could also work for the conventional waterfall approach; however, we have rarely seen frequent recalibration of waterfall projects.

In the situation illustrated in Figure 2.17, the team appears to have underestimated the time required to produce the deliverables. The clue to the real cause of this slippage should arise during the daily sprint meetings. The Scrum Master will have gathered information during these meetings to identify the impediments to the team reaching their objectives. The estimates may have been erroneous or the team may be having interpersonal problems or some portion of the team may be sick.

When the duration estimates are suspect, the Scrum Master, team, and project/product sponsor can decide to reduce some of the product or service content to allow the team to meet the sprint objective. An example of a reduction could be temporary elimination of some features or reducing the scope of other features (depth of feature).

Figure 2.18 shows a team that is executing their sprint activities better than expected. Again, this effect could be due to erroneous estimates or risks that the team had accounted for in the development estimates that never happened. As with underestimation, the scrum approach allows the team, the Scrum Master, and the project/product owner to add scope or content to achieve the reasonable results within the sprint.

This visual representation is what is often referred to as the *empirical* nature of scrum. The slope of the line and the intersection with the *x* axis are the concluding

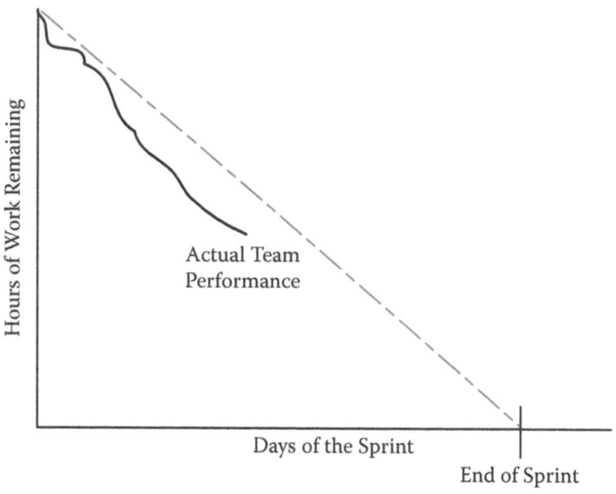

Figure 2.18 Overestimated burndown chart.

time for the sprint. If the slope of this line predicts beyond the sprint closure date, then the sprint is behind schedule. If the slope of the line crosses the *x* axis prior to the expected sprint termination, then the team is ahead of schedule.

2.6.7 Project Budget

One of the benefits of the scrum methodology is that the hours available during each sprint are strictly accounted for. We will compare the hours throughout the project to the available funds/hours for the development. Such an approach makes it possible to predict when the project is approaching a budget overrun and allows for prompt calculation of the remaining budget.

Since the sprint goal is to always have a sellable product at the end of each print, the end of a budget is not necessarily the death of the product. We would simply have a product that did not contain all the features originally laid out or derived at the beginning or during the project. Since development is ongoing and we are delivering a sellable product at every sprint, we have multiple opportunities for revenue generation for the developing organization. We can use this revenue to continue the project; in effect, paying our way as we go.

It is easy to adapt to changes within a project when the budget is on a cost plus firm-fixed-fee (FFF) contract. It becomes challenging when the contract is FFF only. An FFF contract has an impact on how much change or how complete the final product will be when it is delivered, not to mention the fact the FFF contracts put the bulk of the financial risk on the side of the supplier of the service or product. The customer's expectations for change management and budget impacts must be addressed early in the project. To use scrum or some other agile methodology that supports the ability to change but not account for that change in the budget increases

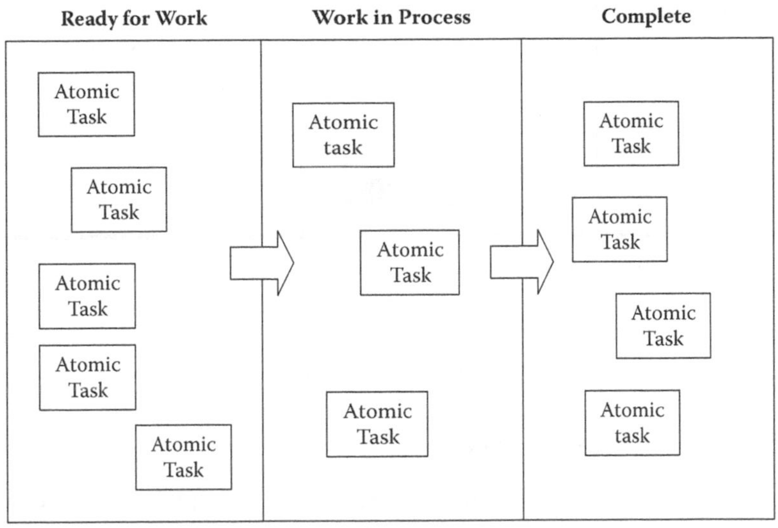

Figure 2.19 Kanban system.

financial risk with each unaccounted for change. The ability to adapt does not mean doing work for free or absorbing all changes. Ultimately how much work gets done is not solely a function of the approach to project change, but the resources and money that allow the development to continue.

2.6.8 Sprint Kanban

Figure 2.19 shows a simple, but effective, setup for starting a kanban pull system with the sprint backlog.

What is going on in this system? In essence, we select "atomic" tasks from the product backlog that we derived from a highly detailed work breakdown structure and put these tasks into a team-accepted sprint backlog. These items go into the first panel of the kanban board. Individual team members can select from the leftmost panel and put the selected items into the work in process panel. We now have a visual indication of queued work, work being performed, and work completed. Of course, the team member will take the completed sticky note and put it into the panel for completed work. The visual system makes maintenance of the burndown chart much easier and provides a somewhat motivational visual cue for the team members. Ambitious teams might use a spreadsheet or some kind of web-based approach to do the same thing. We believe the three-panel hardware is simple and effective for colocated teams. Distributed teams would probably want to use the electronic approach to the kanban system.

The presence of any kanban in the to-be-worked area is a trigger for potential work. Also note that any items that need rework can be moved back to the queueing

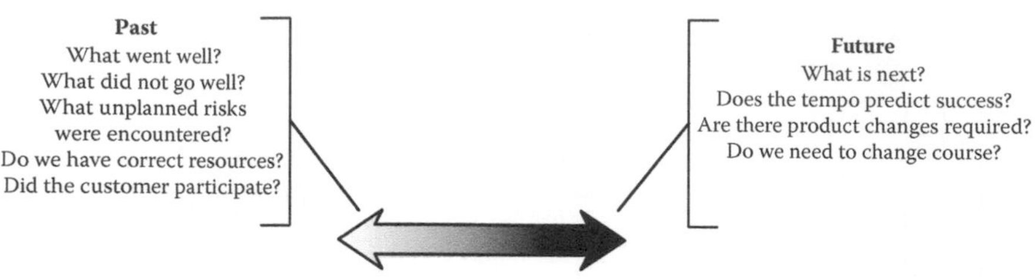

Figure 2.20 Sprint retrospective.

area for renewed selection. It might make sense to add some kind of mark to the sticky note to indicate that it already has been worked on previously.

2.7 Sprint Retrospective

At the end of the sprint is the sprint retrospective. During this time, the project team performs a review of what has happened during the most recent sprint and anticipates the next sprint.

The retrospective is a critique of the most recent past sprint of the team. One approach is to ask ourselves two simple questions: What did we do well? What do we need to improve? Launch process gate reviews and other heavy-handed approaches can be improved by incorporating at least a brief retrospective so that team learning occurs (see Figure 2.20). Our experience with staged-gate processes suggests that once a customer or client has seen a schedule or time line, the schedule is not open to alteration. We suggest that the retrospective allow for both learning and recalibration of the overall project schedule. Software scrum teams will often develop a sprint velocity (or story point velocity) based on empirical measurements of *their specific* team, which allows for calculation of the probable conclusion date for the project or subproject.

For those who think the classical approach is the way to operate, please take a look at a well-baselined timeline with both planned and actual start and finish dates. We normally begin to see variance between plan and reality within the first few weeks of the project, a situation that worsens as the project continues. With the

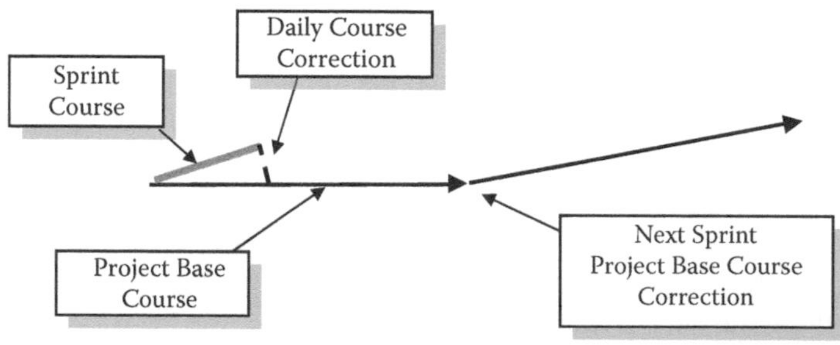

Figure 2.21 Scrum and tempo.

scrum approach, we will update the baseline at every retrospective/planning session and inform the client if the deliverables schedule is at risk (see Figure 2.21).

2.7.1 Meeting Leader

The self-directed work team of scrum allows for rotation of the retrospective leader, who, in most cases, will function as the Scrum Master. While rotation is not a requirement in the scrum approach, it is a reasonable option because it allows more of the team to contribute in a variety of ways while encouraging participation. Additionally, the experience of the responsibility reduces risk by having all members of the team able to pick up the activity when needed. In most meetings, the meeting leader is really a facilitator rather than a directive-oriented traditional manager.

> As a retrospective facilitator you may follow the content, but your primary responsibility is the process. When facilitators talk about process, they aren't talking about a heavyweight metrology . . . . Retrospective leaders focus on the process and structure of the retrospective. They attend to the needs and dynamics of the group and help the group reach a goal. Retrospective leaders remain neutral in discussions, even when they have strong opinions.[2]

2.7.2 Meeting Etiquette

All effective, efficient meetings have rules of etiquette for their execution such as behavioral requirements, agendas, minutes, and preparation. The goal of scrum is to maximize the ability of the project to meet the demands of the customer. As such, we use meeting tools to avoid spending time on poorly led or ineptly scoped meetings that detract from the ability of the team to meet project demands. Often this has more of an impact than the one-hour meeting that was scheduled as the team members leave the meeting bewildered by the wasted time and lack of results.

To avoid wasting time, we want to be sure that our scrum meetings, be they the daily scrum meetings or the end-of-sprint retrospective/planning meetings, are highly-focused, short, and have the following characteristics:

- Time-boxed
- Goal-driven
- Action oriented

Like most scrum practices, concision defines the process. Our experience in endless meetings suggests that getting to the point is more likely to motivate attendance than long-winded orations and fumbled non-agendas. The smarter team members come to the daily scrum meeting prepared to answer the three questions succinctly (What occurred yesterday? Today? What obstacles?) The time-box can only be broken by request of a member and consensus from the rest. Table 2.2 shows one example of a sprint retrospective.[3]

Table 2.2 Retrospective Sequence

Task	*Percentage of Time (%)*	*Time (min)*
Set the stage	5	6
Gather data	30–50	40
Generate insights	20–30	25
Decide what to do	15–20	20
Close the retrospective	10	12
Total	100	120

Source: Derby, E. and Larsen, D. *Agile Retrospectives, Making Good Teams Great*, The Pragmatic Bookshelf, Raleigh, NC, 2006, 19.

2.8 Iterative Product Delivery

At the end of each sprint, the goal is to have a deliverable product that is sellable. Obviously, we may not see a real product develop in the first few sprints since the product is moving from nonexistence to some level of functionality. However, the intent is to deliver a functional product to the customer with every release. What this means is that the organization that is providing the investment to produce the product will already be receiving payback on the development money even while the product development is under way (assuming we are receiving purchase orders for the delivered prototypes/products). This approach also results in a substantial reduction in risk since the product is always in some kind of condition for release. Additionally, the customer/client can exercise the product to determine if it meets specifications or if it has any unsavory behaviors.

By now, the observant reader should notice the metaphorical parallels between the scrum approach to managing time and lean manufacturing. Daily sprint meetings and semi-monthly or monthly retrospectives and sprint planning meetings shorten the duration between iterations, very much like level loading and one-piece flow in lean manufacturing. If a production line is properly level-loaded, the manufacturer should always have *some* product to deliver even if it is not the entire lot (known as split-lot delivery), since something is usually better than nothing.

2.8.1 Payback Period

One measure of project success is how long it takes for the developing organization to recover their investment. When the product has multiple deliveries that can be sold, we see opportunities to begin receiving revenue for the product. This desirable situation starts the payback period even while the development work is ongoing. Ultimately, these iterations will shorten the product payback period, often within a few sprint periods (see Figure 2.22).

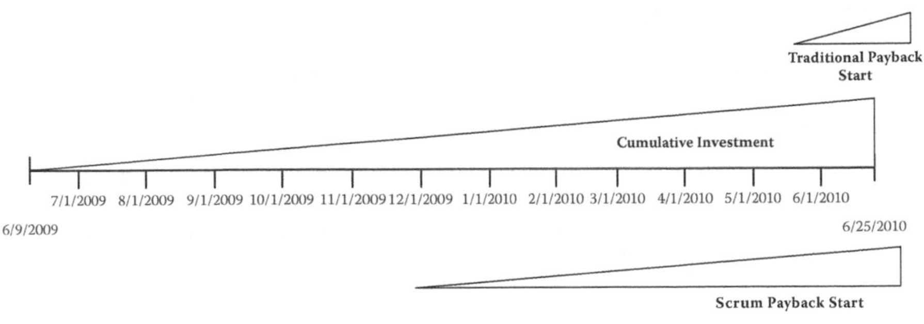

Figure 2.22 Example of payback impact of scrum.

It is important to note that scrum will only be expeditious if the objectives can be achieved in the short-term. Long lead-time items such as design-from-scratch hardware are more difficult to achieve using the scrum approach, although the product development can certainly be decomposed sufficiently to allow for a scrum-type approach to product delivery. These obstacles can be overcome through the use of commercial-off-the-shelf (COTS) hardware, modular hardware design philosophies, or extensive use of simulation. Alternatively, we can break the long lead-time item into smaller increments and apply the scrum approach to the subsystems.

If the project duration is substantial, we will probably want to use a more sophisticated approach to payback. The discounted payback takes into account the interest rates involved, although it makes the calculation of the payback period somewhat more complex. The two tables that follow show the difference between simple payback and discounted payback. With simple payback (Table 2.3), we see repayment in five years, whereas with discounted payback (Table 2.4), we see our repayment sometime in year seven.

COTS means using a hardware product that has already been developed. This requires identification and analysis by the customer and determination of the final application of the product. Even though the hardware is outsourced, it still plays a role in achieving the customer's or the organization's objectives so it must be given adequate attention.

A modular hardware design philosophy speeds the hardware development to match the scrum tempo. In this case, the designing organization creates the subassemblies of the hardwares so that the developers can reuse these portions of the

Table 2.3 Simple Payback

Cash flow	5,000
Initial expense	25,000
Payback, in years	5

Table 2.4 Discounted Payback

Year	*Cash Flow*	*Multiplier*	*Discounted Flow*	*Result*
0	−25,000	1	−25,000	−25,000
1	5,000	0.909	4,545	−20,455
2	5,000	0.826	4,130	−16,325
3	5,000	0.751	3,755	−12,570
4	5,000	0.683	3,415	−9,155
5	5,000	0.621	3,105	−6,050
6	5,000	0.564	2,820	−3,230
7	5,000	0.513	2,565	−665
8	5,000	0.467	2,335	1,670

design for subsequent designs. By eliminating some of the design cycles through reuse, we accelerate throughput. No matter which choice we make, the velocity may be dominated by the slowest design portion.

The lack of availability of hardware early in the process can be overcome through extensive use of simulation. The sprints themselves can be used to provide oversight for developing the models for the simulation. It is also possible to inject the simulation during the later sprints when we have assembled models. We can use simulation at any level, from the creation of the first working model to the final system. We recommend that scrum teams consider the benefit of simulation:

- Early tryout of ideas
- Damage-free exercise of the product
- Quick turnaround
- Coordination with the customer/client
- Examination of extreme scenarios

2.8.2 Return on Investment

Return on investment is another measure of how successful a project is monetarily: It is the ratio of the money generated as a result of the project to the amount of money invested to produce the product. Again, earlier payback can improve the business case for the development activities since we have revenue generated even as the product is undergoing development. Earlier payback goes beyond simple return on investment by improving on the net present value of the project by improving on the payout (negative cash flow) taken for non-recurrent engineering at the very beginning of the project. Cash flow moves in the desired direction much earlier when we can invoice for existing development during the project rather than waiting for the terminus of the project timeline.

What follows is a simple example of a return on investment calculation.

$$\frac{Return}{Investment} = \%ROI$$

$$\frac{20{,}000}{100{,}000} = 0.2$$

2.8.3 Internal Rate of Return

The internal rate of return (IRR) is the net present value (NPV) of the project with the NPV set to zero and the discount rate calculated instead of the dollar value; in other words, we are calculating the interest rate rather than some dollar value. The primary defect of this approach is the lack of scalability when comparing projects with significant resource differences. Our example shows an initial investment of 100 units with a cash flow of 120 for one period of time. We calculate the IRR to be 20%. Often, enterprises will set hurdle rates for the IRR calculation to force a cut-off point where the project is considered to be unsatisfactory.

$$For\ IRR\ NPV = 0$$

$$-100 + \frac{120}{[(1 + \frac{IRR}{100})^1]} = 0$$

$$\frac{120}{[(1 + \frac{IRR}{100})^1]} = 100$$

$$\frac{120}{100} = \left(1 + \frac{IRR}{100}\right)^1$$

$$1.2 = 1 + \frac{IRR}{100}$$

$$1.2 - 1 = \frac{IRR}{100}$$

$$0.2 \times 100 = IRR$$

$$IRR = 20$$

2.8.4 Sunk Costs

Sunk costs are costs that have already been incurred and cannot be recovered. An example of this might occur during a staged gate approach, in which the end of each phase looks back and forward in time to determine if the project should continue. The money already spent to the date of the review are sunk costs. The participants in the gate must consider if the spent money and project state warrants a continuation of financing for the next phase of the project. If the project is canceled, the money that we invested is lost—generally with no hope of return.

The problem with sunk costs occurs during some projects when managers attempt to remove the money already expended in the updates of the IRR or ROI calculations. This action inflates the business case by allocating the previous costs as sunk costs and resetting the calculation from this gate forward.

2.9 Burndown Chart and Scope Changes

We can use the scrum approach to help manage scope change. In general, modifications and adaptations will occur as both the scrum team and the customer learn about the new product or discover new desires and needs. However, acceptance does not mean that these changes should be ignored. The burndown chart can keep track of scope changes as well as the progress being made. In Figure 2.23, the scope additions are illustrated by the bars on the graphic below the x axis. As usual, the frequent meetings and control mechanisms of the scrum approach allow us to manage scope changes realistically rather than pretending that some miracle is going to shorten a critical path.

2.10 Meetings

Scrum meetings occur every day. The manager meets with the team for a brief period. The period for each team member can be as little as two to five minutes. The manager (also known as the Scrum Master) will ask, at a minimum, three very simple questions:

- What did you accomplish yesterday?
  - The individual will enumerate objective items completed on the previous workday.
  - The focus is on *accomplishment*, not completion of "busy work."
- What are you accomplishing today?
- What are the obstacles you are encountering?

While other questions and discussions are not specifically forbidden, we try to remember that meetings are cost centers and time spent on them is often time wasted. Furthermore, by keeping the time box very short for the scrum meetings, we increase the likelihood of attendance, since the participants do not feel that they

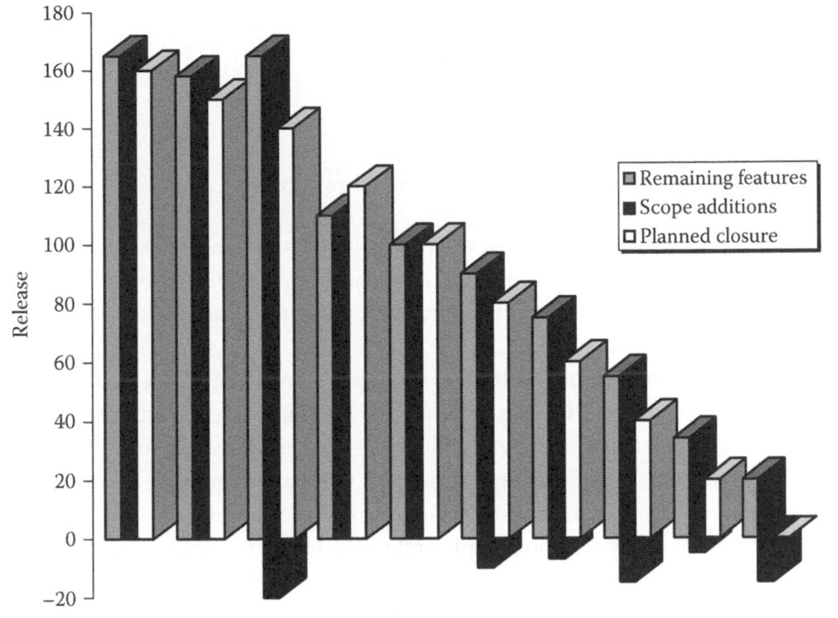

Figure 2.23 Example of burndown chart with scope additions.

are wasting their time. We encourage complete attendance by all team members because a specific member may learn something from another member that propels the sprint forward.

Under no circumstances should a scrum meeting be punitive. The purpose of the meeting is to update task completion information for participants as well as surfacing any obstacles that may be reducing the effectiveness of the downstream team or of the overall department. While not a requirement, minutes are not detrimental to the daily scrum meeting and they can provide documented evidence of progress for higher-level management. These minutes also provide for a kind of "virtual" scrum for members who were unable to attend.

Virtual scrum allows members of a team to update each other by answering the three questions using e-mail. With this approach, members with remote devices like BlackBerry smartphones can participate and update other team members. We have found this particularly effective with the test and evaluation management team, especially when a member is traveling. The e-mail is very simple and looks like the following:

Yesterday

- Finished X
- Started Y
- Planned Z

Today
- Finishing Y
- Starting Z

Obstacles
- Inadequate funding for a complete Z
- Management doesn't understand need for testing for Y

Each member will send an e-mail with a similar format. Since all members understand the general concept, these e-mails are very brief and to the point. Sometimes they function even better than the face-to-face meeting because they do not lend themselves to idle chatter.

The third question, about obstacles, reflects a somewhat different approach to control during project or line management. This approach reflects the idea that removing obstacles to performance—allowing the employee to function as they naturally would—is a more powerful approach than implementing controls. Some industries (automotive, pharmaceuticals, food) implement "controls" as a central part of their product management philosophy/religion. The first reaction to an untoward event is the implementation of a new control, rather than investigating the situation for a barrier to superior performance and removing that barrier. Even the military may have fewer "controls" than these three industries.

2.11 Project Human Resources

The secret to success in a scrum project lies with the tempo delivered by the team. Fisher identifies the phases an organization goes through on the way to developing Self Directed Work Teams.[4]

1. Investigation
2. Preparation
3. Implementation
4. Transition
5. Maturation

Let's see how Fisher's approach relates to scrum. We check to see what happened during the previous period, usually a day. We check to see what is going on during the current period, usually today. We then ask what it would take to remove impediments to improve performance. We track progress using a burndown chart based on estimates made by the participants themselves. At all times, we are treating our team members like adults rather than like children. At no point do we give ourselves the illusion of some kind of abstract control. The goal is to stay in touch with reality. Moreover, Fisher's concepts of preparation and implementation occur during the commencement of scrum usage. Transition occurs quickly on the way to maturation.

2.11.1 Scrum Master

The team is the central focus of scrum. However, another key participant is the Scrum Master. The Scrum Master has many responsibilities, a few of which are listed below.

1. Remove obstacles
2. Facilitate conflict resolution (team hygiene)
3. Ensure adherence to the scrum and team rules
4. Acquire resources
5. Keep the team focused (no external distractions)

To keep things moving, the Scrum Master fills many roles, not the least of which is to keep the team focused on objectives, as well as monitoring the work results using the burndown chart and daily reviews. The Scrum Master is to the team as the project manager is to the project.

One of the most important responsibilities of the Scrum Master is to make sure that the team environment is one that is optimal for production for the team and to make sure the team knows the objectives and the operating box for the project:[5]

> Instead of controlling specific team member activities, for example, team leaders clarify the boundary conditions within which team activities are performed. These boundaries include things like project costs, schedules, or customer requirements. In much the same way as managing by principles, this provides people the autonomy required to generate personal commitment instead of the robotic compliance that is generated by externally imposed controls. It also obsoletes the requirements for many externally imposed controls like supervision, policies, and procedures.

2.11.2 Teams

J. Richard Hackman identifies the four essential features of a real team in *Leading Teams: Setting the Stage for Great Performances.*[6]

1. Team task
2. Clear boundaries
3. Clear specified authority to manage their own work processes
4. Membership stability over time

Scrum project management places great emphasis on team interactions as opposed to individual performance. The book *Creating Teams with an Edge* identifies three attributes to determining if the task requires an individual or a team:[7]

- Task complexity
- Task interdependence
- Task objectives

When we have used the scrum approach, the team worked in the same facility. Different discipline or department members had easy access to a small meeting room useful for the daily scrum meeting. The product and sprint backlogs were easily distributed through e-mail. To a large extent, the scrum teams were self-directed, with minimal management intervention and on those occasions, primarily used to remove sprint obstacles. Also, the close collaboration and progress tracking differentiated both the stellar contributors and the slackers. In short, we had an ideal situation.

When a team is spread across multiple locations, sometimes multiple nations, the scrum team meetings can become more problematic. However, even when we are not dealing with an ideal situation, we see no reason why technology can't be used to mitigate the geographical separation.

2.11.3 Team Roles

We define roles seen in the scrum literature to be consistent with these definitions while adding our own twist.

One of the scrum categories is the "pig." The name "pig" comes from an old saw, where when it comes to cooking, the pig is *committed*, but the chicken is *involved* (eggs).

2.11.3.1 Pig

2.11.3.1.1 Product Owner

The product owner represents the voice of the customer. He or she verifies that the team works effectively from the business point of view; in short, the product owner will see to it that the business case for the product backlog and the sprints actually make good business sense. The product owners concern themselves with customer-oriented items (user stories in software development), and then set priorities and often update the product backlog.

2.11.3.1.2 Scrum Master

The Scrum Master drives the scrum activity, especially in the beginning of the project. Their principal job is to counteract obstacles to task completion. This person is generally not the leader of the team except in the beginning, since we expect team emergence as the practice becomes self-reinforcing, although we expect the Scrum Master to insist that the daily scrum occur and be well attended. The Scrum Master is very much like the function of a Champion in the Six Sigma approach to quality improvement. They ensure that the scrum process is used as intended. As a facilitator, the Scrum Master will keep the various scrum activities on task by invoking the appropriate rules and procedures.

2.11.3.1.3 Team

The team is chartered to deliver the product, process, or service. A team is often composed of five to nine cross-functional individuals with appropriate skills. We call this the "team-as-composed." The real team is an emergent phenomenon based on common goals and shared risks.

2.11.3.2 Chicken

2.11.3.2.1 Users

Users are the individuals for whom we develop the product. In some cases, we might use the term "end user" to indicate intervening levels of customers and suppliers. In the automotive world, we use the word "tiers" to refer to the different levels, with the primary supplier being the "Tier 1" supplier.

2.11.3.2.2 Stakeholders

Stakeholders are people for whom the project has some kind of impact. They can be team members, customers, suppliers, managers, internal customers, internal suppliers, the surrounding community—anybody for which this particular project has relevance. Stakeholders may participate in sprint reviews, but are usually not involved in day-to-day activities or charting.

2.11.3.2.3 Managers

Managers have functional responsibilities for different development disciplines (in development at least). They are often process owners as well and they own the environment in which the team functions. In many cases, the manager may function as the Scrum Master, although this approach seems to militate against self-formation of the team.

Notes

1. James Grenning, "Planning Poker," (2002), `www.objectmentor.com/resources/articles/PlanningPoker.zip`, accessed 29 December 2009
2. Esther Derby and Diana Larsen, *Agile Retrospectives, Making Good Teams Great,* (Raleigh, NC: The Pragmatic Bookshelf, 2006), 29
3. Esther Derby and Diana Larsen, *Agile Retrospectives, Making Good Teams Great,* (Raleigh, NC: The Pragmatic Bookshelf, 2006), 19
4. Kimball Fisher, *Leading Self-Directed Work Teams* (New York, NY: McGraw-Hill, 1993), 165
5. Kimball Fisher, *Leading Self-Directed Work Teams,* (New York, NY: McGraw-Hill, 1993), 169
6. J. Richard Hackman, *Leading Teams: Setting the Stage for Great Performances,* (Boston, MA: Harvard Business School Press, 2002) 37–60
7. Richard Leucke, *Creating Teams with an Edge,* (Boston, MA: Harvard Business School Press, 2004), 9

Chapter 3

Scrum and Conventional Project Management

It is easy to see the dismay that arises with conventional project management. These projects are often populated with already-late tasks and team members that identify problems—yet these deadbeat disasters receive a paltry proactive action from the project manager. It is difficult to say if conventional practices fail because the practice is invalid when the execution of the process is often so unsatisfactory.

The processes may be different but the fundamentals and the objectives are similar (see Table 3.1). For example, before any project can progress, the team must know the scope and the objectives of the project. That scope, as we have seen, can be contained in a well-constructed work breakdown structure and then deployed to the team regardless of the project management philosophy.

Conventional project management differs first from scrum project management in the planning phase. At a minimum, the activities required to produce the scope of the project are planned by this phase. For a large program, this phase can consist of months of activities. Under the conventional modality, the project will be planned from the start to the delivery date and usually documented using a software tool like Microsoft Project. Figure 3.1 shows some generic phases for a conventional project; most staged-gate types of project bear a family resemblance regardless of the actual names of the gates and phases.

3.1 What Is the White Book?

At the conclusion of the project, although sometimes at the end of each project phase in the life cycle, we review our successes and failures. Feedback is drawn from the team on the challenges and actions taken by the team that produced good results.

Table 3.1 Comparison of Conventional and Scrum Approaches

Conventional	*Scrum*
Earned value	Burndown chart
Work breakdown structure	Product backlog
Communications plan	Daily sprint meetings
White book	Retrospective
Gates	Releases

There can be discussions of novel methods of handling the risks of the project, unexpected or unanticipated events, and controlling actions taken.

This information is then recorded in a "book" that allows subsequent project managers to learn from the past without having to relive the same actions and failures. The white book is designed to facilitate organizational learning regarding project management and processes the organizations used to deliver the projects. Often the focus is on the failures more than the successes. The tricky portion of compiling such a white book is to keep it from becoming a compilation of petty complaints.

3.2 Project Backlog–Scope

Any activity or task that is not complete is, by definition, part of a backlog. The standard project time line tools show this status clearly with percentage complete indicators and sometimes illustrate these states with dark completion lines on the Gantt charts. With the scrum approach, we are moving the tasks from the relatively inflexible project time line into a product backlog and thence to a sprint backlog. The only risk with the backlog tracking lies in the lack of dependency information, although we see no reason why this information cannot be included in a spreadsheet or a database.

3.3 Project Burndown Chart

We already mentioned the burndown chart, both for schedule and for budget. A mature conventional project manager will most likely already be performing earned value analyses on his or her projects. Adding the burndown chart simply adds an

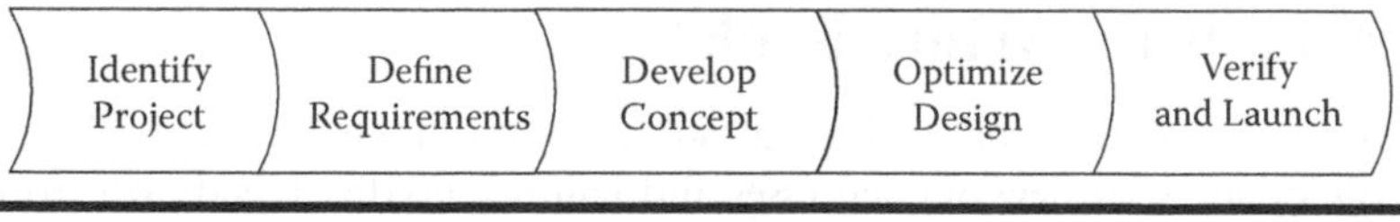

Figure 3.1 Example traditional project phases.

excellent graphical representation of status, useful to both the project team and upstream management.

In essence, whether we practice scrum management or conventional project management, we still have to ask three questions:

- What is our variance to budget?
- What is our variance to schedule?
- What is our variance against quality expectations?

These three questions refer to the "sacred" triad of cost, delivery, and quality. Success on these three items derives from better than adequate management of human resources, logistics (materials and supply), configuration, technical performance, and many others.

The scrum approach adds to conventional project management by increasing the tempo of reporting while simultaneously increasing the tempo of accomplishment. The increase in pace reduces risk to budget and schedule due to the lack of overruns and because of solid reporting practices. With the scrum approach, we are using brief daily meetings to achieve updates instead of weekly or biweekly meetings. As the team becomes accustomed to the new approach, they begin to achieve a momentum of their own and the need for heavy-handed management fades as they become self-maintaining. If we are truly fortunate, a real and sustainable team will emerge to become something greater than the skills of the constituent members might indicate.

3.3.1 Time Management

In any method of project management, time management is fundamental. With conventional project management, the assessment of time performance occurs when we compare the schedule to the actual performance (see Figure 3.2). Sometimes, we do this by using systems that capture hours billed to specific work breakdown structure elements. However, we can have serious logistical challenges with these systems; for example, we can expect latency in time reporting—that is, how we synchronize the time reporting to the project schedule. Furthermore, we can have the additional difficulty of erroneously charged time against work breakdown structure elements.

With scrum applications, the time slice is compressed and more easily controlled. The team and the project manager have daily exchanges, which reduces latency issues. The project manager and the team are focused on a specific set of tasks listed in the sprint backlog and the collaboration is well-scoped to assure an attainable completion within the sprint period to which the team has committed, adding to the quality of the time-expended data. In short, the accelerated response rate results in improved data resolution and accuracy with the added benefit of a daily audit through the scrum meeting.

We advocate the use of rigid time-boxing to control time during any meeting. When time-boxing, we set a hard deadline for the end of the task, which in many cases will be the meetings. We have gone so far as to use a countdown stopwatch or

Figure 3.2 Conventional project management.

digital kitchen timers to keep the meeting within time boundaries. In our experience, project management team meetings often last an hour to an hour and a half and take place weekly; during project management team meetings, much time is wasted with late arrivals, irrelevant chatter, and agenda-free fumbling. With the daily scrum meeting, we ask participants to respond only to the three questions with less than three minutes per person. This way, it is very easy to work for fifteen minutes with five managers and then release them. In essence, by performing meeting "liposuction," we save money for our enterprise.

The team can also use the time-boxing approach to control the amount of time allotted to various tasks. The use of countdown timers improves the cadence of the activity and may lead to ahead-of-schedule completion for some of the tasks. We use time-boxes for everything from meetings to routine tasks to one-of-a-kind tasks (with some variance). We can time-box even the simplest tasks to enhance our mindfulness of the time we waste.

3.3.2 Communications

When using conventional project management methods, we might develop a detailed communications plan—we have rarely seen these documents used except in the case where we developed them ourselves. The communications plan defines stakeholders and the preferred method of disseminating information and possibly the format in which to present the project status.

There may also be a resource allocation matrix to clarify who is responsible for what areas, and who is consulted in other areas (see Figure 3.3).

	Component2 SW	Component2 HW	Project Manager	Component1 SW	Component1 HW	System Spec	System Verification	Tools	Manufacturing	After Market	Training	Tech-Pubs
Design Doc												
Component2	A	A	In	In	In	In	In	In				
Systems	In	In	In	In	In	A	In	In				
Component1	In	In	In	A	A	In	In	In				
Component2 Release												
Hardware		A	In	C	C		C	In	C	In	In	In
Software	A		In	C	C		C	In	C	In	In	In
Component1 Release												
Hardware	C		In	A			C	In	C	In	In	In
Software		C	In		A		C	In	C	In	In	In
Testing												
Component2	A	A		In	In		In					
Component1	In	In		A	A		In					
Systems	In	In		In	In		A					
Training												
Component2		A	A							R	R	R
Component1				A	A					R	R	R
Systems						A				R	R	R

Accountable	**A**
Participant	**P**
Review Required	**R**
Input Required	**I**
Sign Off Required	**S**
Informed	**In**
Consulted	**C**

Component2 SW	RD
Component2 HW	SR
Project Manager	AC
Component1 - SW	MB
Component1 - HW	MB
Systems Spec	WC
System Verification	MM
Tools	JG
Manufacturing	BW
Aftermarket	SR
Training	BB
Tech-Pubs	LO

Figure 3.3 Resource allocation matrix.

Meetings may (or may not) be scheduled on a monthly basis or some other recurring schedule. Teams that are colocated may have impromptu meetings that are used to resolve last minute open issues. Those that are cross-scheduled will take on a very large scope and consume a significant amount of time. The project participants will likely represent the cross-functional nature of the project and have these various area representatives cycled through as required. Of course, in the scrum approach that we propose, the team members would meet for a brief, time-boxed duration every day!

3.4 Relation of Backlog to Work Breakdown Structure

The product backlog is derived from what we call the "work breakdown structure" in conventional project terms. The typical software product backlog may not have an obvious hierarchy to it; however, it is not difficult to modify the document to reflect the breakdown. One excellent way to show the breakdown as well as the "atomic" level items is to use a spreadsheet functionally decomposed from left to right and then choose only the rightmost items for the product backlog or for the sprint. This sheet can be adjusted to suit individual needs. Everything we already know about work breakdown structure development already applies to the scrum approach. The only significant difference occurs when we break tasks down to the "atomic" level.

A work breakdown structure can be defined to be:

- A product-oriented hierarchy composed of hardware, software, services, data, and facilities.
- A description of the product, or products, to be developed and/or produced; in so doing it relates the elements of work to each other and to the end product.
- An expression of a natural hierarchy down to any level of concern.

The Department of Defense generally recommends three levels to the hierarchy; we recommend much more detail because the result of this effort allows daily management of delivery of the various products. MIL-HDBK-881 recommends the following items for the work breakdown structure:

- Integration, assembly, test, and checkout efforts
- Systems engineering and program management
- Training
  - Equipment
  - Services
  - Facilities
- Data
  - Technical publications
  - Engineering data
  - Management data

  - Support data
  - Data depository
- System test and evaluation
  - Development test and evaluation
  - Operational test and evaluation
  - Mock-ups
  - Test and evaluation support
  - Test facilities
- Peculiar support equipment (items not currently in inventory and must be developed)
  - Test and measurement equipment
  - Support and handling equipment
- Common support equipment (items currently in inventory)
  - Test and measurement equipment
  - Support and handling equipment
- Operational and site activation
  - System assembly, installation, and activation
  - Checkout on site
  - Contractor technical support
  - Site construction
  - Site/ship/vehicle conversion (obviously military and defined as what must be done to accommodate the product—on the civilian side we would look for opportunities for reuse)
- Industrial facilities
  - Construction/conversion/expansion
  - Equipment acquisition or modernization
  - Maintenance (industrial facilities)
- Initial spares and repair parts

3.4.1 Work Breakdown Structure Is a Direct Reflection of Requirements

With either approach—conventional or scrum—the voice of the customer is the driving mechanism for the scope of work which, in turn, drives the requirements. It does not matter if the requirements come from external sources or if they are internally derived. When requirements change, the work breakdown structure changes because the work breakdown structure is precisely a decomposition of top-level deliverable elements. With the scrum approach, replanning is simplified because we are dealing with a few weeks or a month planning horizon rather than a monster-sized, multi-year Gantt chart from a program management tool.

The work breakdown structure is important to both conventional and scrum project management styles and line management because the cost centers are always derived from project deliverable elements (so much so that it is easy to develop templates for the work breakdown structure). The concept works because products are composed of systems which, in turn, are composed of subsystems and then components and so on. If we start with a top-level assembly as the first or second level on the work breakdown structure, we can easily break the product down into "atomic" level tasks. The same approach will apply if we are dealing with other deliverables such as internal specifications, models, failure mode and effects analyses, and the round of documents that our quality system requires.

3.4.2 Modifying Work Breakdown Structure to Reflect Changing Requirements

Tracking updates to the project scope or changing deliverables to meet requirements is where many projects go astray. Lack of change management or inept configuration control makes it difficult to compare what you have with what you expected or needed. With scrum, we derive the product backlog directly from the work breakdown structure. Why can't we use the work breakdown structure as our product backlog? The answer lies in the specific use of these tools: the work breakdown structure is a formal document designed to support cost and schedule reporting as part of a contract; the sprint backlog does not have to be so formal, although we can still track costs and schedule. Also, in the product and sprint backlogs, we often will not see the higher-level deliverables as such, since we are focused on the "atomic" tasks that lead to them.

3.4.3 How Deep Should the Work Breakdown Structure Go?

The work breakdown structure will deconstruct as far as we need to go such that we can put items into the appropriate sprints. What we mean is that if we have a fifteen-day sprint, then we have to have tasks that can be accomplished during that period. We call this highly detailed analysis "atomic" decomposition because we are decomposing the upstream tasks until further decomposition no longer makes sense. When we complete this task, we will have a list of "atoms" that become part of the sprint backlogs.

In some cases, the "atoms" will be small enough so that we can complete them within minutes. In our experience with a production testing group, this approach removed the excuse that "we didn't have time to do this work." By putting these small tasks in the sprint backlog, we could drive some level of accomplishment through the completion of these micromovements.

3.5 Task Decomposition to "Atomic" Level

As we have indicated, "atomic" decomposition occurs when we take a work breakdown structure down to the level where task completion becomes binary—either it is done or it isn't done. If we are truly clever, we may even break our tasks down to the point where they have roughly equivalent durations, allowing for the use of story points. The reason for doing this is manifold:

- We provide immediate gratification and, thus, reinforcement to our project team.
- We can roll-up completed tasks into a conventional project management program and get a "percentage complete" result suitable for passing on to management.
- We can easily insert these low-level tasks into even the shortest sprint backlog.

We use this approach to work breakdown structure decomposition in order to ensure completion of *all* tasks. The cost center decomposition ensures that we identify dependencies and include them in our sprints. Nothing about the sprint approach precludes the use of conventional project management tools. We feel, however, for relatively small or simple projects, the spreadsheet list and burn-down charts are probably adequate. Our goal is to remain flexible and lightweight, rather than burdening ourselves with a lumbering, uninspired approach to our task list.

3.6 Sprint

The sprint, in scrum terms, is the primary miniplan derived from the overall plan, which, in the scrum case, happens to be the product backlog. These periods last typically between a fortnight to a month. We recommend that this duration be consistent and relatively inflexible throughout the project. We don't advise extending beyond one month per sprint unless there are extenuating circumstances. The rationale, at least in part, arises from the recurrent reviews with the team. The frequent auditing that occurs with the daily scrum meetings and the sprint retrospective/planning meetings create the possibility of the project team becoming much more adaptable to demands and changes in the external environment. Prolonging the sprint looks more like conventional project management, slowing down the response.

3.6.1 Sprint Review

The sprint review serves a similar role to the gate reviews and the white book exercise. The exception is from a white book perspective anyway; there is time to act on the findings of the review. Unlike white book reviews (lessons learned reviews) that happen at the end of a project and get tucked away never to be seen again, what is learned during one sprint is used to improve subsequent sprint performance. Unlike gate reviews, sprint reviews repeat like a heartbeat—they are not abstractly scheduled as is the case with many staged-gate approaches. Consequently, we see cascading learning through the duration of a project.

3.6.1.1 Managing Congested Backlogs

For each sprint, we have identified the activities to deliver the specific sprint items from each element in order of priority in the product backlog. Sometimes the team will overestimate their ability to complete candidate tasks for the next sprint and "stuff" the sprint with too many activities. We find this situation occurs when some of the team members are hot-dogging for an influential manager.

In order to manage the congestion, we must know that we are congested. This situation becomes immediately apparent in the burndown chart as the completed hours drop way below the expected completion rate. The only rational solution to this situation occurs when we begin to eliminate items from this sprint and set them up for the next sprint backlog. In many cases, the team can solve the problem by themselves; at other times, involvement by the Scrum Master or other management intervention may be necessary to delete the appropriate items.

Burndown charts provide the visual system that allows team members to assess progress by themselves and promotes the concept of a self-directed work team. The Scrum Master should use good judgment before requiring intervention by management. Allowing the team to solve the problem for themselves provides for group learning.

3.6.2 Creating New Sprints

We generate new sprints using the content and priorities determined by the product backlog. We continue the process for as long as we have a product backlog. We can add to the product backlog at any time during the development process, often with new customer input and direction. Because the product backlog is somewhat of a moving target, we have another reason for using the much shorter sprint approach.

The sprint backlogs are always derived from the product backlogs. When we update the product backlog with new or altered tasks, we affect all subsequent sprints. Once again, the analog with one-piece flow in the lean factory approaches holds true with the sprint backlog—we lose little because we are configured to adapt to change.

3.7 Effect of Scrum on (Velocity) Tempo

Because tasks in the sprint backlog have commitments from the team, we can expect the tempo of closure to increase. We found that in a three-month period, we were able to cut a product backlog list in half even though other tasks were being added to the product backlog during this time. Before the introduction of the scrum approach, this product backlog (if we can call it that) generally ran in steady state at approximately sixty tasks, largely because most of the projects never received enough focus to arrive at closure. After using the scrum approach for approximately six months, the list of steady state tasks varied between fifteen and thirty.

3.8 Command and Control

Command and control is a misunderstood concept. We should not confuse command and control management with autocratic decision-making by miserable managers. The command and control approach in its simplest form is a control system where the control portion is the feedback loop and the command portion is the result of the comparator (decision-making device or person). The scrum approach is also a control system, although the "comparator" is less distinct than in the traditional command and control philosophy of many militaries.

The scrum approach bears somewhat of a resemblance to the management of the Israeli Defense Force, where decisions often occur through self-directed work teams rather than waiting for a manager (upstream officer) to make the choice. This form of command and control provides for significant flexibility as well as adaptability to changing circumstances. Our goal is to avoid getting locked into project or line decisions made months or years before the issue at hand.

In the scrum approach as we have described it, autocratic management is out of place. Once the team becomes accustomed to the simplicity and brevity of the daily scrum meetings, direct management diminishes substantially.

3.8.1 Communications

One of the great strengths in scrum project management lies with the enhanced communications. One model for the number of communications channels[1] required for a given project can be defined using the equation:

$$\textit{Number of communications channels} = \frac{N \times (N-1)}{2}$$

For conventional projects, the calculation can yield a large number. At nine project members, we already need seventy-nine channels to communicate. With a smaller scrum team of six persons, we would only have thirty-four channels or less than half of those needed by the project team. Keep in mind that some large projects may have hundreds of team members at various times throughout the project, so the conventional approach can easily suffer from communication collapses as the system becomes so complicated that it is unmanageable.

The graphic on the left in Figure 3.4, shows some of the channels possible in a conventional project. We see a lot of informal communications occurring in the background and many difficult-to-coordinate links. The more distributed and the larger the team, the more difficult coordination becomes. The right side of the figure shows the reduction in channels brought about by using the scrum approach. Richard Luecke pointed out that

> One of the great and commonplace failures of organizational life is the failure to share information. Someone knows something that could help a coworker but does not think to share it. A department has information

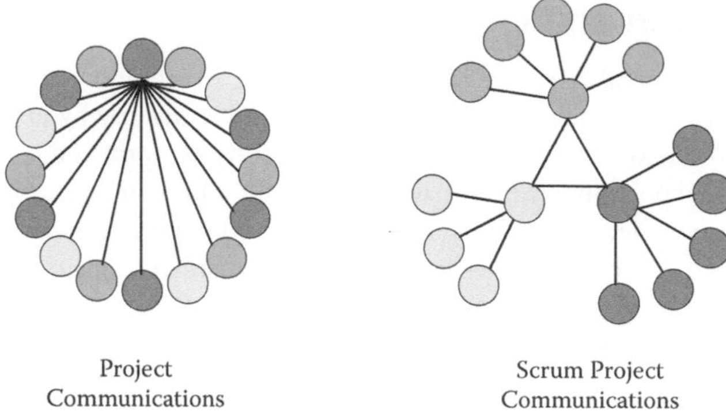

Figure 3.4 Compare typical project to scrum project communications.

in its database that, if combined with data held by another department, would produce a revelation.[2]

3.8.2 High-Speed Throughput

Customers can interact easily with scrum teams. We can enhance the probability of delivering a desirable product by making the customer part of the team. Obviously, we desire to control customer influence to the point that we are not making undocumented and hasty decisions as well as contributing to uncontrolled scope creep. In other venues such as military contracts, customer-supplier fraternization may be controlled by contractual requirements that, in some cases, make engineer-to-engineer communications for work illegal!

On the other hand, by soliciting comments from and interacting with the customer, we are able to make modifications to the product or service so that we can more optimally reflect the design intent from the customer's point of view. We can establish protocols for customer communication early in the project in order to avoid scope creep. In reality, scope creep is often a reflection of poor project management practice. Figure 3.5 shows our team interacting with a customer in a kind of dialogue.

3.9 Quality

Experience suggests that the project overlords will try to crash (shorten traumatically) the test schedule toward the end of the project. Generally, what happens is that developmental items begin to see schedule slips as requirements change and we find out our duration estimates are wrong. The cumulative effect of schedule slips is to extend the development phase at the expense of any validation and verification activities, assuming that the final delivery date does not shift. Not surprisingly, this

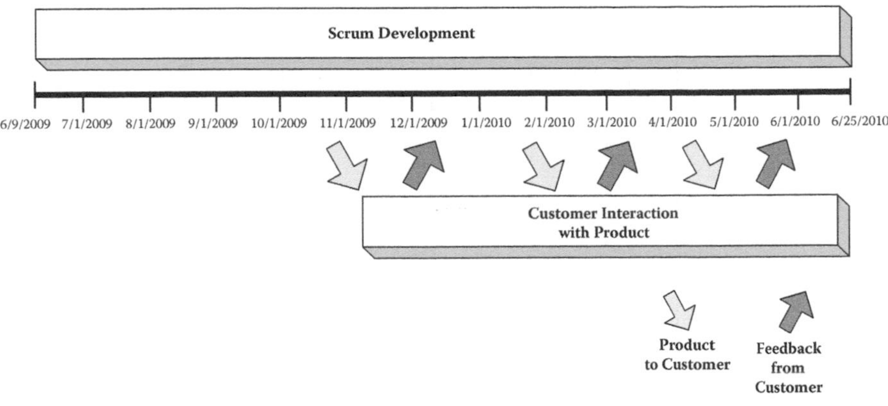

Figure 3.5 Quick turns and quality.

situation may lead to abbreviated testing if management or the customer refuses to push out the delivery date to accommodate verification and validation. We have seen more than a few incidents where companies have released products to an arbitrary delivery date while being aware that the product had known issues.

3.9.1 Product Testing

Scrum's cyclic approach, with each sprint delivering a functional product, also requires verification that the product does indeed meet specified requirements, as well as any derived requirements. These are *sellable* products that require testing before delivery. With conventional product development, the testing of the product often ends up at the end of the product development—just before delivery to the customer. If software or hardware deliverables are dilatory, the delivery date is seriously compromised due to shortening of the test regime. This is not usually the path the project manager will take. The only other alternative is to deliver a product that is only partially tested, leaving product quality at risk and threatening the supplier with potential lawsuits when the product fails in the field. This situation has an impact on the product maintenance cost, with numerous corrective actions needed to deliver the quality the customer expects. Figure 3.6 is a part of a traceability matrix, showing how test cases correspond to system-level requirements. A complete traceability matrix can be huge since it must represent how each test case or set of test cases corresponds to each requirement, explicit or derived. The number of test cases can easily grow into the tens of thousands, requiring a substantial investment of time, money, and people in the development of automated test stands.

With enlightened scrum project management, the customer will participate intensely in the development process. Keeping the customer involved during the development effort means the customer is not likely to be surprised by the end result

Requirements		Sys_Req 1.0	Sys_Req 1.1	Sys_Req 1.2	Sys_Req 1.3	Sys_Req 2.0	Sys_Req 2.1	Sys_Req 2.2	Sys_Req 3.0	Sys_Req 3.1	Sys_Req 3.2	Sys_Req 3.3	Sys_Req 3.4
TC 1.1	3	1			1		1				1		
TC 1.2	3		1			1			1				
TC 1.3	1			1									
TC 1.4	2				1		1						
TC 1.5	2									1			1
TC 2.1	1												1
TC 2.2	4	1				1		1				1	
TC 2.3	3				1	1	1						
TC 2.4	1				1								
TC 2.5	1		1										
TC 2.6	3	1							1			1	
TC 2.7	3			1						1	1		
TC 3.1	5	1	1		1	1		1					
TC 3.2	1												1
TC 3.3	1											1	

Figure 3.6 Requirements and product testing.

Requirements		Sys_Req 1.0	Sys_Req 1.1	Sys_Req 1.2	Sys_Req 1.3	Sys_Req 2.0	Sys_Req 2.1	Sys_Req 2.2	Sys_Req 3.0	Sys_Req 3.1	Sys_Req 3.2	Sys_Req 3.3	Sys_Req 3.4
TC 3.4	1	1											
TC 3.5	1			1									
TC 3.6	3					1		1	1				
TC 4.1	1									1			
TC 4.2	2										1	1	
TC 4.3	4	1			1		1						1
Test Cases	46												

Figure 3.6 Requirements and product testing. (*Continued*)

of the development effort. Additionally, those areas that are poorly defined can be made more concrete by allowing the customer to interact with the design team during the iterations of the design. Ultimately, whatever we call quality is in the eyes of the customer. Thanks to tooling costs and outmoded project philosophies, it is uncommon to see quick turns of the product and functionality delivered to the customer regularly. In most conventional models, much of the design documentation must be in place prior to the development execution. With the scrum approach, the customer adds or alters functions and performance based on feedback or actual use or trials of the product. Additionally, the multiple, iterative releases make it possible to critique the output of the project team and redirect the project effort into a more desirable direction.

3.10 Use of Existing Project Management Tools

The scrum approach, much like any other form of project management, requires an understanding of the details of the work and knowledge of where we are within that continuum at any given time. With this knowledge we will know when the project is displaying undesirable schedule or budget deviations. The standard project management tools can be used by scrum teams to their advantage, while providing documentation for upstream managers who may not understand how scrum works.

3.10.1 Earned Value Management

Earned value management techniques are not unique to either traditional project management or scrum project management. This technique was born from Department of Defense; however, the technique applies any time the team makes the effort to estimate the work and track the work results to plan (see Figure 3.7).

3.10.1.1 Planned Value

Planned value is the sum of all of the costs of the project up front. This summation establishes a time and expenditure rate, allowing those monitoring the project to determine if they are on the predicted spending track (see Figure 3.8). This is the baseline for project expenditure.

The planned value illustrated in the figure is derived from a conventional project. This figure illustrates the seemingly ubiquitous "S" curve of the cumulative expenditures of the project. The lower portion of the "S" is what we typically see during the planning phase of the project. The long linear portion of the curve is associated with the execution and control portion of the project leading to delivery of the product. We associate the final curve of the "S" with the closing activities of the project. For a scrum project, the cumulative curve will be largely linear, since each work period is essentially the hours available for the scrum team.

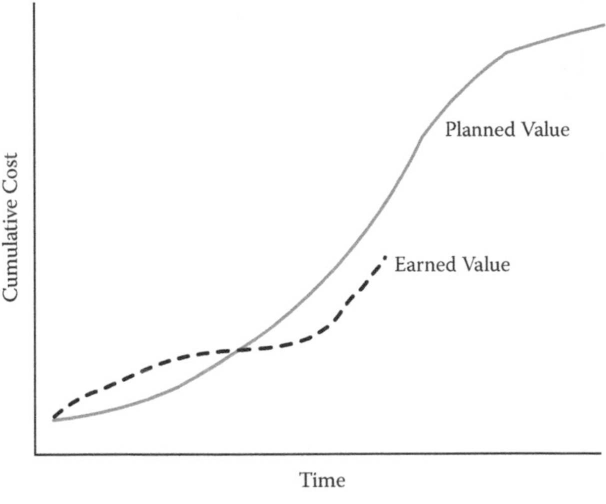

Figure 3.7 Earned value management.

3.10.1.2 Earned Value

Earned value is also known as Budgeted Cost Work Performed (BCWP). This is the amount of value earned for specific work progress by the project. Stated another way, this is the amount accomplished as a reflection of the dollar amount spent. Let's say we have a specific task that has a budget of $30,000. Monitoring the task, we find that we are 25% complete. We can use this to determine the amount spent on

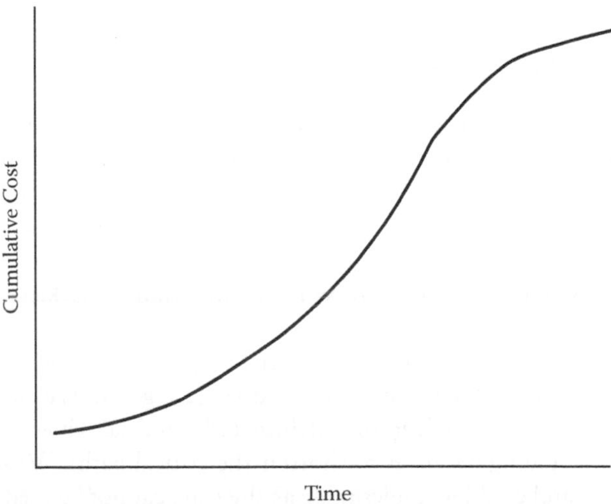

Figure 3.8 Planned value.

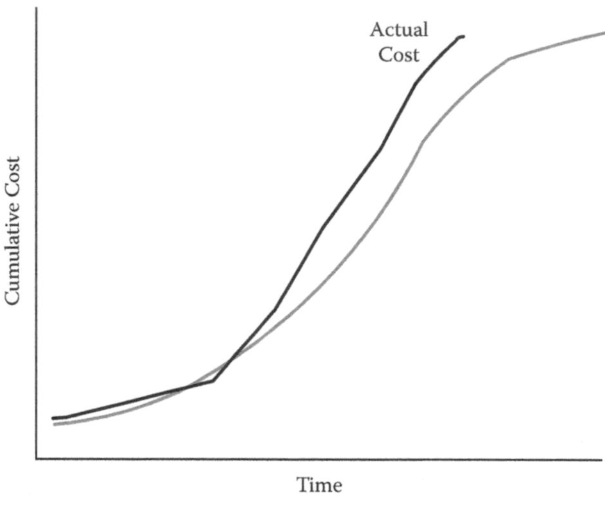

Figure 3.9 Actual cost.

this effort:

$$\frac{\$30{,}000}{0.25} = \$7{,}500$$

3.10.1.3 Actual Cost

The actual cost is the cost it has taken the project to deliver at any point during the project (see Figure 3.9).

3.10.2 Critical Path Method

In conventional project management, the critical path is composed of the longest, slackless, consecutive task durations of the project. This amounts to the shortest time the project could be delivered and meet expectations (see Figure 3.10). To be able to use this technique, the project manager must know all of the tasks required and the durations of those tasks. Additionally, the project manager must know the dependencies between tasks. Any increase in the duration of slackless tasks extends the project delivery date.

Knowing these task dependencies and the critical path allows the project manager to make decisions about how best to achieve project goals. We might use such emergency actions as *fast tracking* (paralleling tasks and activities to shorten the path) or *crashing* (adding resources to shorten the critical path). We see no reason why fast-tracking and crashing, undesirable as they are, cannot be used in the scrum approach. If nothing else, they will benefit from the intense auditing and improved communications among our scrum teams.

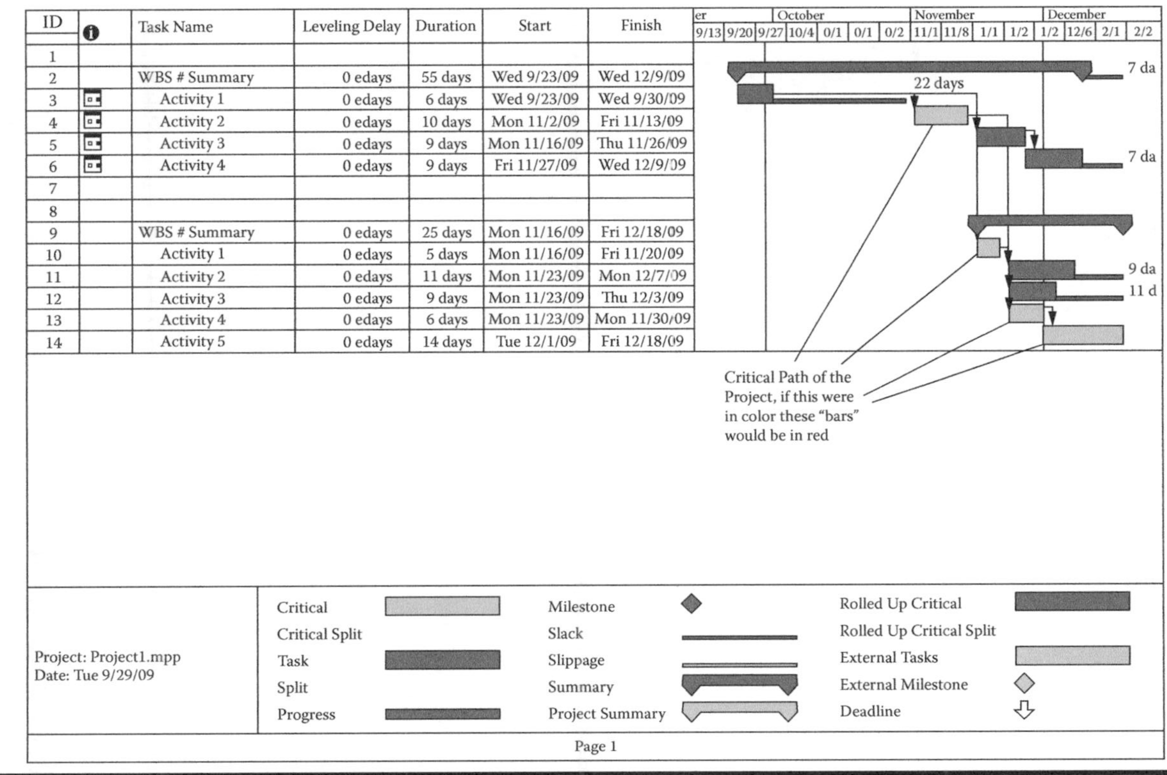

ID		Task Name	Leveling Delay	Duration	Start	Finish
1						
2		WBS # Summary	0 edays	55 days	Wed 9/23/09	Wed 12/9/09
3		Activity 1	0 edays	6 days	Wed 9/23/09	Wed 9/30/09
4		Activity 2	0 edays	10 days	Mon 11/2/09	Fri 11/13/09
5		Activity 3	0 edays	9 days	Mon 11/16/09	Thu 11/26/09
6		Activity 4	0 edays	9 days	Fri 11/27/09	Wed 12/9/09
7						
8						
9		WBS # Summary	0 edays	25 days	Mon 11/16/09	Fri 12/18/09
10		Activity 1	0 edays	5 days	Mon 11/16/09	Fri 11/20/09
11		Activity 2	0 edays	11 days	Mon 11/23/09	Mon 12/7/09
12		Activity 3	0 edays	9 days	Mon 11/23/09	Thu 12/3/09
13		Activity 4	0 edays	6 days	Mon 11/23/09	Mon 11/30/09
14		Activity 5	0 edays	14 days	Tue 12/1/09	Fri 12/18/09

Figure 3.10 Example of critical path.

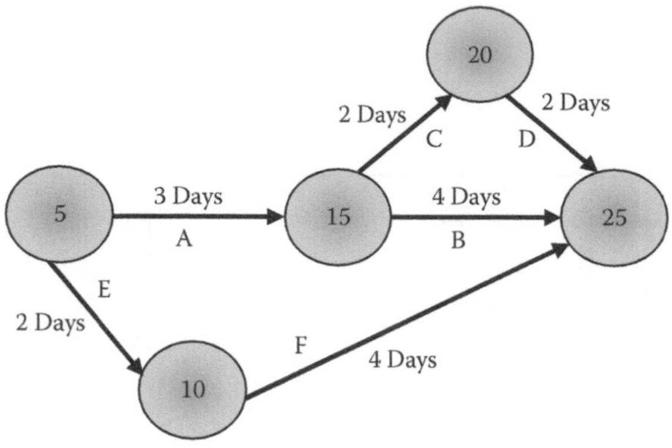

Figure 3.11 Example of PERT.

3.10.3 PERT

Project Evaluation and Review Technique (PERT) is a method of schedule development. The tasks that are required to generate a specific deliverable (work product or product backlog) are manipulated in terms of order of execution with the goal being to minimize the amount of time to deliver the final product. This method could be employed as preparation for the upcoming sprint. The priority-ordered product backlog is modified such that the team will determine the tasks that must be undertaken to achieve these sprint deliverable items. The tasks are then reworked using the PERT approach to streamline the dependencies (see Figure 3.11).

3.10.4 Gantt Charts

Gantt charts are a common tool for communicating tasks and responsibilities in conventional project management. We lay out the tasks in order of start dates and represent durations with a bar chart. Since a true Gantt chart does not represent task dependencies, the tool is mainly useful for communication only. It is much weaker than a network diagram, which does indeed show dependencies among tasks.

In the last decade, some of the project management softwares have produced a hybrid chart, the improved Gantt chart. In this chart, the dependencies can be seen in the graphical portion and other information such as percentage of completion is also rendered (see Figure 3.12).

3.11 Risk Management

Risk management methods are largely the same regardless of the project methodology. The end goal is to reduce the impact or remove the possibility of things that can impact the project's success. We accomplish the goal through risk identification, risk elimination (when possible), and risk mitigation.

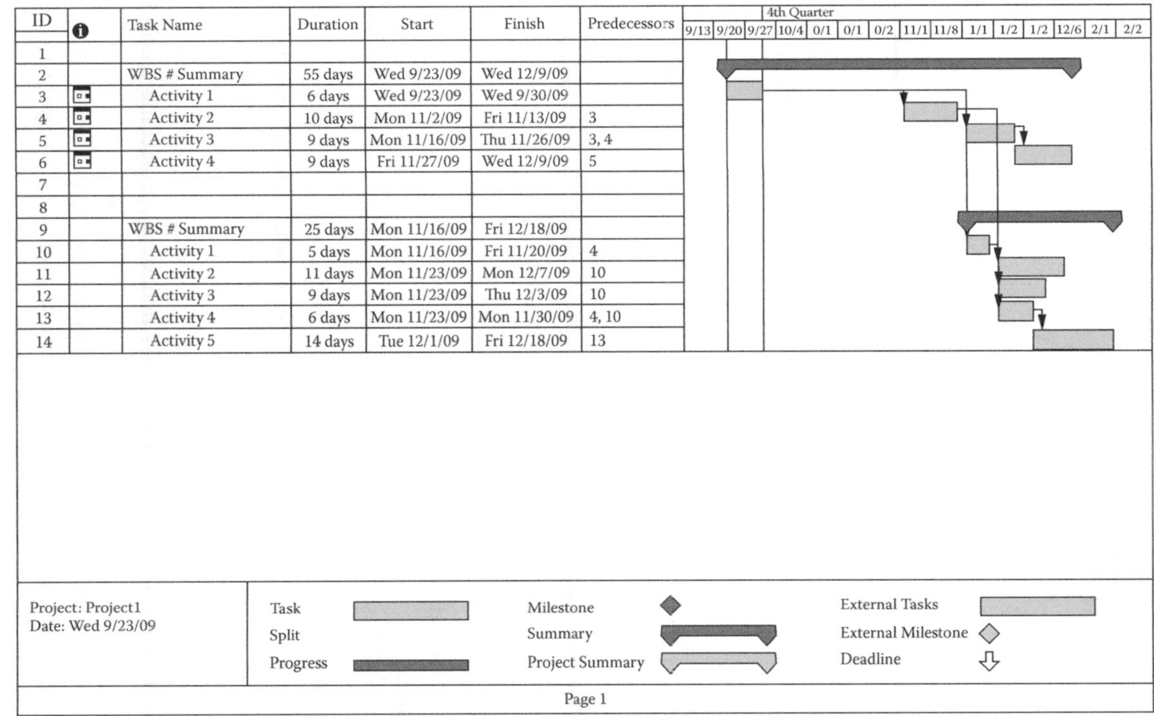

ID		Task Name	Duration	Start	Finish	Predecessors
1						
2		WBS # Summary	55 days	Wed 9/23/09	Wed 12/9/09	
3		Activity 1	6 days	Wed 9/23/09	Wed 9/30/09	
4		Activity 2	10 days	Mon 11/2/09	Fri 11/13/09	3
5		Activity 3	9 days	Mon 11/16/09	Thu 11/26/09	3, 4
6		Activity 4	9 days	Fri 11/27/09	Wed 12/9/09	5
7						
8						
9		WBS # Summary	25 days	Mon 11/16/09	Fri 12/18/09	
10		Activity 1	5 days	Mon 11/16/09	Fri 11/20/09	4
11		Activity 2	11 days	Mon 11/23/09	Mon 12/7/09	10
12		Activity 3	9 days	Mon 11/23/09	Thu 12/3/09	10
13		Activity 4	6 days	Mon 11/23/09	Mon 11/30/09	4, 10
14		Activity 5	14 days	Tue 12/1/09	Fri 12/18/09	13

Figure 3.12 Example of a Gantt chart.

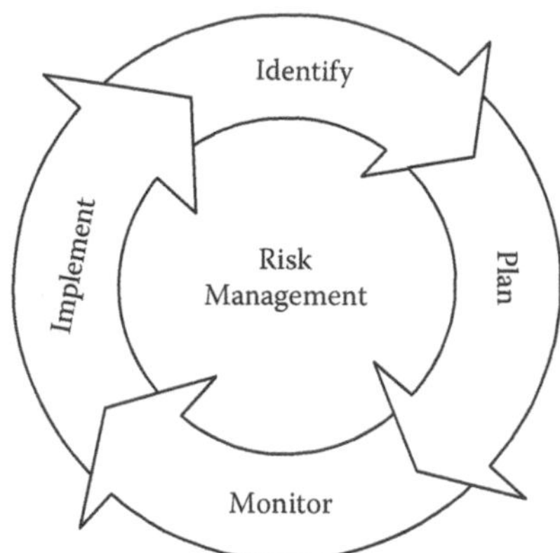

Figure 3.13 Risk management process.

The following list presents the process we might use to manage risk (see Figure 3.13):

- Identify
  - Quantify risk
  - Qualify risk
- Plan
  - Mitigation actions
  - Identification of unacceptable risk thresholds
  - Risk responsibility
- Monitor
  - Boundary spanning
- Implement
  - Threshold crossed—plan and take action

While we would like to believe that conventional project managers perform detailed investigations of those things that could go wrong, experience suggests that this activity often does not benefit from much effort on their part. Too many times, the project manager and team will be surprised by unexpected actions during the course of the project. Nevertheless, in traditional projects, the project manager and team brainstorm to identify as many risks as they believe the project may encounter. They can do this either by project phase or through completion of the project. With either choice, the period of risk impact under scrutiny is weeks or months. If the risks are reviewed by phase, each phase of the traditional project may require a renewed investigation of the risks for that upcoming phase.

In scrum, the risk review happens at each sprint and during each scrum session. As road blocks come in view, the team works to overcome them. The review of distant future impacts, while interesting, is not as significant as those activities that lie within the current planning horizon. We are not advocating deliberate avoidance

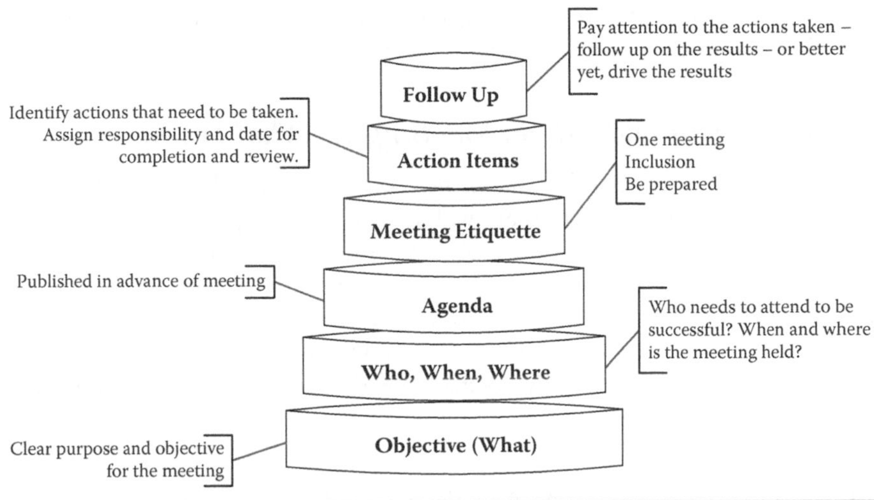

Figure 3.14 Meetings.

of downstream risk, but we are suggesting that risk management is built into the scrum framework to begin with.

3.12 Meetings

Meetings are a necessary and costly evil in any project method, which suggests the time spent in meetings should be reduced. Meetings are an extension of the communications of any project and communication is key to delivering what is required and expected (see Figure 3.14). With the scrum approach, meetings have a predetermined time-box. In practice, we use a kitchen timer to keep the team on track. The "stand up" nature of the scrum meetings helps reduce the possibility of the meeting becoming excessively long.

Teams will also find internal obstacles such as processes and noncommunicative organizational structures called silos. They will also find mental constraints and prejudgments that go along with these obstacles. These are all exacerbated by either too many nonproductive meetings or lack of meetings altogether.

With the scrum approach, the meetings all have a recurring theme, the agenda is fixed, and all project participants know the rules. The meetings are frequent (daily and at the end of a sprint) and short. Problems are identified quickly and communicated throughout the project.

3.12.1 Setting up Meetings and Times

We set the daily scrum meetings for the same time every day. This behavior makes attendance habitual, which will facilitate attendance and preparedness for the meeting. The daily scrum meeting is mandatory, with the only alternative being virtual scrum through e-mail. We are trying to get our team members to communicate with each other to improve opportunities for synergy.

3.12.2 Who Should Attend Meetings at What Level?

The daily sprint meetings should have the entire team and the Scrum Master in attendance. Sometimes, the customer will attend if the corporate rules allow this level of participation; however, the customer shouldn't be a distraction, dragging the focus away from the immediate tasks and deliverables at hand but, rather, an honored team member. When the customer needs to understand some nuisances of the project or product in detail, the discussion should be taken directly to the Scrum Master. Discussions or activities that draw the team away from the impending deliveries should be eliminated.

3.12.3 What Documents Are Essential?

In order to balance speed, quality, and information distribution, we need critical evaluation of the documentation. For the daily scrum meeting, no document is essential. For the sprint retrospective, we would like to see the following documents:

- An updated product backlog
- The most recent sprint backlog and results
- The most recent burndown chart
- A template for the next sprint backlog
- A list of any items that are rolling over from the previous sprint

We attempt to keep the roll-over items to a minimum since they represent inaccurate estimation of task durations or poor understanding of task dependencies.

3.12.4 Effects on Tempo and When They Occur

Since meetings often present non-valued-added time, they represent an opportunity for improvement. We can use a stopwatch or some other timer (e.g., kitchen timer) to set a time-box all can see and use the shortened time to enact Parkinson's Principle in the opposite direction from which we normally think of this rule—instead of allowing work to expand to fill the time allotted, we force the work to contract to fill the shorter time allocated.

Time-boxing is a way to motivate us to spend less time milling around and more time adding value. We can time-box the following business activities, for example:

- Meetings
- Meals
- Phone calls
- E-mail reading

- E-mail writing
- Employee evaluations
- Site tours

We could expand on this list, but the point is obvious: If we reduce wasted time, we will be consistently adding value. Apply this concept to the scrum team and we multiply the value.

3.12.5 Risk Reduction

Focused meetings allow for risk reduction via communications between or among the development parties. These meetings can include suppliers as well as customers, both internal and external. A meeting such as we are describing would gather the entire supply chain, allowing for some cross-pollination of ideas. Additionally, these gatherings also provide a forum for the customer to promptly manage any open issues.

Kim Heldman, in her book *Project Manager's Spotlight on Risk Management*, says "communicating is the most important responsibility you have as a project manager. Ninety percent of your time is spent in this activity. I can think of no other activity that has a greater impact on project success."[3]

By accelerating the frequency of meetings, but containing them with abbreviated time-boxes, we are enhancing communication all the way up and down the supply chain. The same results occur when we handle our communication meetings internally using the same techniques.

3.12.6 Challenges and How to Overcome Them

3.12.6.1 Lack of Attendance

The need for strong participation is more critical in the scrum approach than it is with traditional project management. The Scrum Master will speak each day in a high-intensity, high-speed meeting. Interchange of information occurs naturally and quickly and oftentimes, team members will effortlessly recombine to manage resource deficiencies such as missing workers.

We found that using a simple Pareto chart for attendance tracking makes it obvious who the nonparticipants really are. Furthermore, when we post it in an obvious location, we don't even have to say anything to the guilty parties directly. However, we shouldn't have to go this far with team members—early successes, short meetings, and focus reinforce participation.

3.12.6.2 Poor Backlog Documentation

The speed of the development is determined in part by the knowledge of the scope of the project. This knowledge originates in the product backlog—at least that is where the product scope is documented. When the backlog information is not clear or is insufficient, the team must constantly stop to generate at least enough of a backlog for the next sprint. The failure to develop a solid product backlog and maintain it delays project activities, but may not in itself be catastrophic to the development team's objectives.

What do we find when we do root cause analyses on half-formed product backlogs? The following list provides some examples:

- The team did not properly develop the work breakdown structure.
- Customer involvement in requirements capture was insufficient.
- The team did not understand the product backlog concept.
- The team was accustomed to ad hoc decision-making.
- Upper management is not supporting the scrum approach.

Of the listed items, the last one can be deadly. While it is possible to execute the scrum approach covertly, the initiative is more likely to succeed with management support.

In a nutshell, the product backlog process should follow these simple steps:

1. Receive or develop a product or service specification
2. Parse out the requirements
3. Derive any ancillary requirements
4. Identify top-level deliverable items
5. Use top-level deliverable items as top-level work breakdown structure elements
6. Decompose work breakdown structure to the atomic level
7. Use the atoms to populate the product backlog
8. Repeat as changes occur to the project

3.12.6.3 Poor Sprint Documentation

We should only see an inadequate sprint backlog if we haven't done the initial work on the product backlog. We need to have a fully developed sprint backlog in order to estimate hours of work per "atom" so that we can represent the goal on the burndown chart. It is the difference between hour estimates and hours actual that generates the burndown chart image of our progress.

3.12.6.4 Lack of Reviews

In essence, when we are using scrum, we have two classes of reviews: the daily scrum meeting and the sprint retrospective/planning review at the end/beginning of each sprint duration. The daily scrum meeting is a lightweight thread, whereas the sprint meeting is a heavyweight process. If we apply the scrum approach with the required tools (daily meeting, sprint meeting), lack of reviews should never be a cause for a breakdown in performance. One of the main points of the scrum approach is that we should never get into a situation where lack of knowledge is causing project problems.

3.12.6.5 Atomization Difficulties

It is difficult to estimate the amount of time it takes to achieve a certain deliverable or product backlog without knowing the goal. Atomizing the work breakdown structure accomplishes at least X objectives:

1. Provides a brief task for use in the sprints
2. Allows for binary done/not-done reporting of completion, which allows project management software to represent percentage completion using a hierarchical roll-up
3. Makes estimation of task duration easier
4. Makes it unlikely that a given atom will extend beyond the end of the immediate sprint duration

Since we will measure our results using the burndown chart, we should encounter no major surprises. If our estimates are completely inaccurate, we will see the failure in the burndown chart as a significant deviation. In order to produce a sellable product by the end of the sprint, we will need to coordinate the atoms well enough so that we have something to sell.

We can coordinate the atoms by visualizing the product as a set of concentric rings or as a set of sets. The innermost ring is the core product (hardware or software) in minimum configuration. The core product provides the first release of sellable hardware or software. As we add a new ring or a superset, we produce another version of a sellable product. This approach requires substantial planning and a complete understanding of what constitutes a minimum configuration. The payoff literally occurs as we release sellable products to customer purchase orders and deliver revenue during the development process. Furthermore, the goal of producing sellable products at each sprint reduces our risk because we are never in the middle of a multi-month prototype development that may or may not be rejected by the customer.

3.12.6.6 Incomplete Understanding of Dependencies

In order for our project management software to properly calculate the critical path, we must construct our project, large or small, as a directed graph—a mathematical object with one antecedent-free node (the kickoff) and one consequent-free node (the closing meeting). We must connect all other nodes in our directed graph with at least one antecedent activity and at least one consequent activity. Any task subset of tasks that are not connected this way are called "hangers." If a hanger has no schedule or budget dependency, then we might ask ourselves why we are executing the tasks immediately; after all, the hanger task is not dependent on anything else.

Dependencies are important in the scrum approach because we need to execute some tasks before we can execute other tasks. Using the directed graph (project management software) can help us develop this network diagram as well as provide a mathematically correct critical path analysis. We need to beware of software that clutters up the screen with alleged critical paths—if the network has not been designed as we have described, we are looking at visual noise.

The atomic level work breakdown structure helps to eliminate the situation where we have missing tasks. Most project management software allows us to organize our directed graph hierarchically, representing the higher levels as "roll-ups." On inspection, we should find no roll-ups with missing tasks or disconnected tasks.

Notes

1. C. E. Shannon, "A mathematical theory of communication," *Bell System Technical Journal, vol. 27*, (New York, NY: July and October 1948), 379 and 623
2. Richard Luecke, *Creating Teams with an Edge*, (Boston, MA: Harvard Business School Press, 2004), 97
3. Kim Heldman, *Project Manager's Spotlight on Risk Management*, (San Francisco, CA: Harbor Light Press, 2005), 20

Chapter 4

Complex Program Management

The more complex the project, the more variables and dependencies in the developing organization, the more important is the requirement for clear and frequent communication.

4.1 Scrum of Scrums

The scrum of scrums is a cascading hierarchy of scrum teams. The Scrum Masters, managers, or designates from one level of teams become team members at the next higher level in the hierarchy. This hierarchical concept is not different than a typical organizational chart and it provides a method for decomposing a massive product backlog into management sub-backlogs and their associated sprint backlogs (see Figure 4.1).

4.1.1 Managing Scrum of Scrums

Larger projects require a larger number of resources. The scrum of scrums is used to manage these larger projects. One of the issues with using the scrum approach this way lies in the communication of issues. In general, a scrum of scrums will suffer from many of the communication issues seen in more conventional program and line management. However, at the scrum team level, we expect to see the same level of improved communications as we see with the scrum approach in general. The difficulty with scrum of scrums, as with any multilevel hierarchy, lies with the quantity and quality of the data as we communicate to the higher levels in the

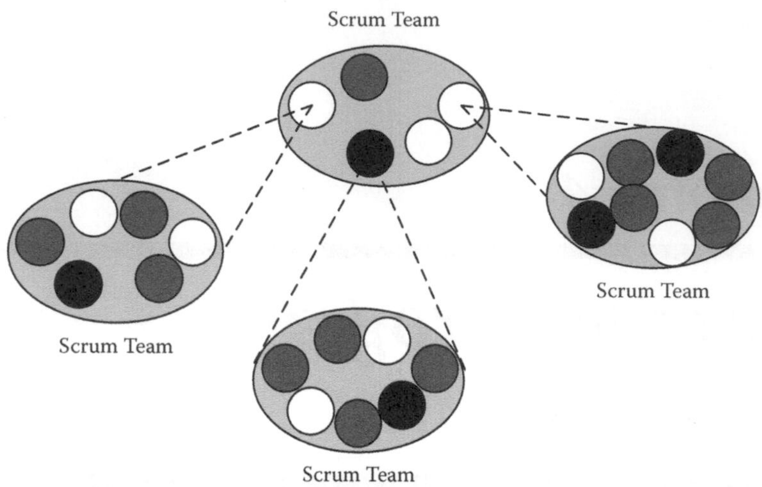

Figure 4.1 Complex systems.

hierarchy; typically, we expect to see attenuation in the quantity of information and a potential loss of quality as well.

The scrum of scrums meeting is an important technique in scaling scrum to large project teams. These meetings allow clusters of teams to discuss their work, focusing especially on areas of overlap and integration. Imagine a perfectly balanced project comprising seven teams each with seven team members. Each of the seven teams would conduct (simultaneously or sequentially) its own daily scrum meeting. Each team would then designate one person to also attend a scrum of scrums meeting (see Figure 4.2). The decision of who to send should belong to the team. Usually the person chosen should be a technical contributor on the team—a programmer, tester, database administrator, designer, and so on—rather than a product owner or Scrum Master.[1]

4.1.2 Reporting Scrum of Scrums

In general, the Scrum Master or line manager is the individual who will take part in the scrum of scrums—at least in the beginning of the project. The scrum of scrum discussions may in time involve topics where it is wise to use other team members as delegates to the next higher scrum in the hierarchy. This scenario can be due to some special experience a certain team member may have, or the area of responsibility the team member has within the project.

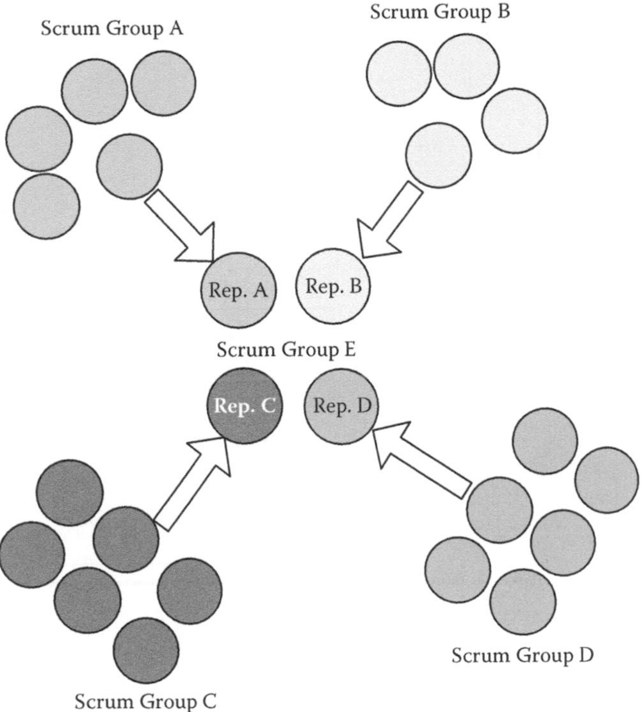

Figure 4.2 Scrum of scrums.

4.2 Budget

We have seen conflict in systems development when the various suppliers have differing philosophies about changes. This unsavory event happens when the waterfall approach is used by some of the developing suppliers and an agile approach like scrum is used by others. When the product requires downstream integration of subsystems, we need to ensure we have a reconcilable response to changes by all suppliers. Firm-fixed-fee suppliers will generally have internal pressure to deliver the least expensive possible product, whereas cost plus firm-fixed-fee suppliers will be able to pass on the cost to their customers. The risk scenarios are significantly different between these types of contracts.

Systems development where there are multiple suppliers or sources of the components for the system will require the budget statuses to flow *up*, as opposed to requirements, which flow *down*. The hierarchical arrangement in the scrum of scrums can be used to pass information up the hierarchy or we can use more conventional cost accounting throughout the project (see Figure 4.3).

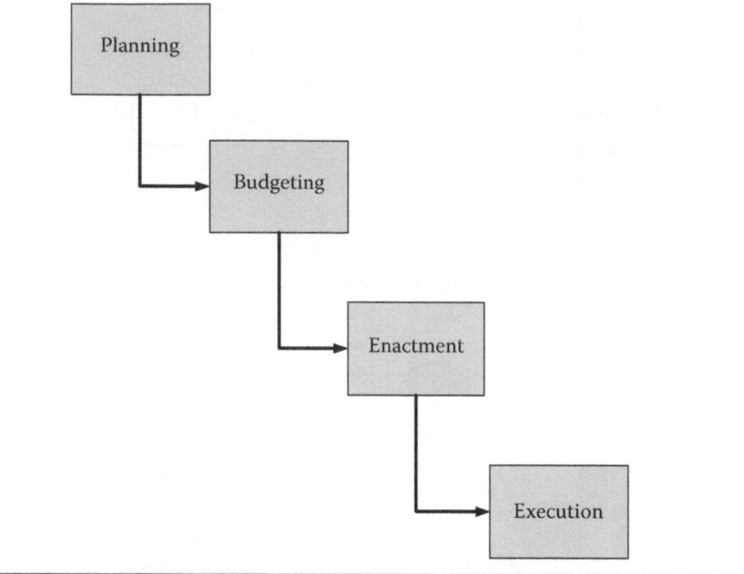

Figure 4.3 Budgets and systems development.

Note

1. Michael Cohn, *Advice on Conducting the Scrum of Scrum Meeting*, (May 2007) `http://www.mountaingoatsoftware.com/articles/35-advice-on-conducting-the-scrum-of-scrums-meeting` (accessed June 10, 2009)

Chapter 5

Scrum and Line Management

5.1 Line Management Tasks versus Project Tasks

It is possible to have a matrix organization where the project manager practices a conventional or waterfall approach, while the line manager employs the scrum approach within the line function. One of us used the scrum approach to manage all product and production test departments. The departmental line managers were the scrum team for the director for the various departments. Within each department, the manager held his or her own scrum meetings. We saw a decline in legacy projects on the product backlog within one quarter and a significant decline (by two thirds) within six months. We can attribute part of this success to eliminating most of the multitasking and focusing on the sprint backlogs.

At the beginning of the process, we selected the projects that were nearly complete for the first sprint. This approach allowed us to remove the easy items immediately. For the next sprint, we chose tasks that were roughly half complete and salted the rest of the sprint with some other atoms. This step allowed us to begin to move tasks with no progress up through the completion list—increasing priority—while still removing the easy-to-complete tasks. As previously untouched projects were included in the sprint backlogs, they became low-hanging fruit also. This systematic approach to choosing priorities was very successful at setting a new tempo for these departments. Figure 5.1 shows how the scrum and sprint meetings line up during line management activities.

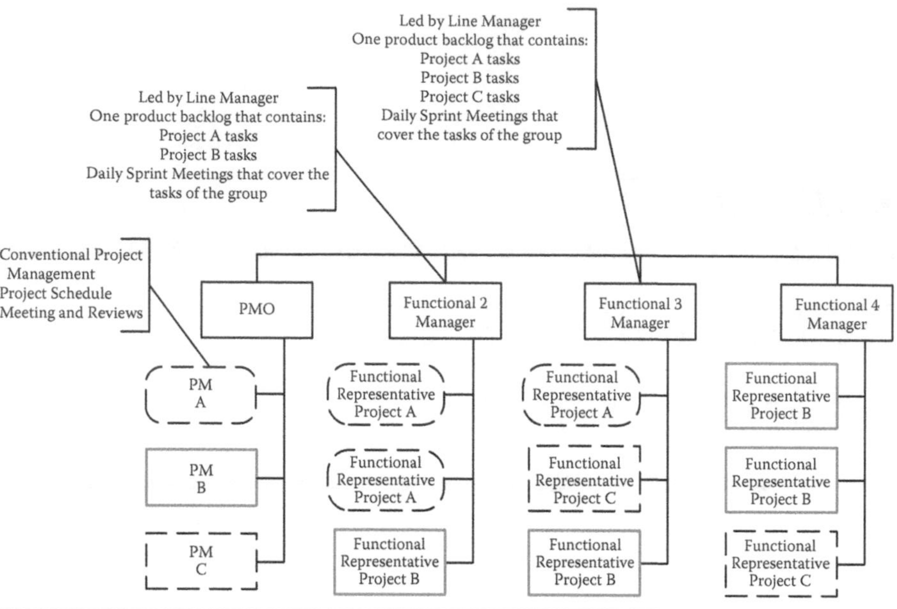

Figure 5.1 Project organization with scrum line management.

5.2 Individual and Team Performance

The concepts that make agile approaches effective have been discussed in management circles for many years. In the book *Putting the One Minute Manager to Work*, by Kenneth Blanchard and Robert Lorber, a system evoking performance from an individual is described in the acronym PRICE:[1]

- Pinpoint—"atomize" the scope
- Record—collect evidence
- Involve—engage the individual or team
- Coach—communicate with the individual or team
- Evaluate—measure, analyze, and report results

While the perspective of the book *Putting the One Minute Manager to Work* is directed at an individual's performance, its application need not stop there. This applies to line management as well as projects, teams as well as individuals.

5.2.1 Pinpoint

We and our teams must identify the scope of the activity and the key measurable performance variables that support our objectives. We won't know what to do if we don't know the objectives, tasks, and subtasks that must occur to meet those objectives. This is analogous to the goal of a project and the tasks it takes to achieve project closure. In the scrum approach, the product backlog drives the scope of the work and activities to achieve the objective. The product backlog is effectively the first level of control.

5.2.2 Record

Whether the activity is line management and individual performance, typical project management or scrum project management, tracking progress toward a defined goal enhances the probability of achieving the objective. Making visible progress toward a defined goal can drive team performance. Results against the sprint backlog are tracked in burndown charts. These charts provide the team with direct feedback on the status of their performance compared to planned performance via quick feedback (not to mention, the daily scrum meetings).

5.2.3 Involve

It is easier to keep the team involved when the team is part of reviews. At each level of scrum meeting, we expect full participation from all team members. The daily scrum meetings are short and informal. The fortnightly or monthly sprint review, planning, and retrospective meetings are somewhat more formal, but not so much as to squelch input from any team member. The hierarchical setup of the scrum meetings also encourages participation at each level with the next level up. The cascading system, if we are using scrum of scrums, allows for participation at each level.

5.2.4 Coach

Some level of coaching will occur during the daily scrum meetings, especially if the Scrum Master is also a line manager. Consequently, the Scrum Master should be prepared for those moments when coaching is appropriate. The actual coaching activity should not occur during the execution of the scrum meeting but, rather, in a private session before or after the daily scrum meeting. The reason for doing this separate session is to avoid potential embarrassment for the team member who receives the coaching.

5.2.5 Evaluate

When we execute an evaluation, we are checking actual team results against planned results. We are not necessarily doing an earned value analysis but, instead, we are executing a portion of the scrum approach. We can evaluate individual team members or the entire team. Clearly, we are most likely to evaluate the team on schedule, budget, and quality. As we have already indicated, we can create a burndown chart for each of these items or have a three-dimensional chart for all of them.

Based on what we have discussed previously about the role of the team in scrum, it should come as no surprise that changes in management methods would require change as well. In Ken Schwaber's book, *The Enterprise and Scrum*, he refers to this change in management method as *servant leadership.*[2]

5.3 Throughput

Increasing throughput requires direction and focus with feedback for those actually doing the work. This feedback is reinforcing to the participants and, more importantly, allows monitoring of the progress to rework the schedule or direction. In most cases, this constant monitoring moves the pace of the deliverables as the team works closer together and as the individuals find the *new groove* of the pace of the expected deliveries.

In Timothy Ferris's book, *The 4-Hour Workweek*, he describes actions taken to control the results of outsourced work.

> **3. I gave him a license to waste time.** This brings us again to damage control. Request a status update after a few hours of work on a task to ensure that the task is both understood and achievable. Some tasks are, after initial attempts, impossible. **4. I set the deadline a week in advance.** Use Parkinson's Law and assign tasks that are to be completed within no more than 72 hours. I have had the best luck with 48 hours and 24 hours.[3]

While this quote is directed at outsourcing, the approach applies to much more than outsourced work including any activity where there is uncertainty and where *we* are not the person required to do the actual work. The tactic espoused in this text is directly comparable to scrum in that the task size is sufficiently small to show progress on an hourly basis and the control portion (feedback) on the status of those tasks can be accomplished quickly and routinely. Figure 5.2 reflects the uncertainties around team performance.

5.4 Movement toward Self-Directed Work Teams

The employee empowerment concept does not mean the manager should ignore the employee. It is fairly easy to make the correlation between the Scrum Master and the line manager for a given group. The increased autonomy of self-directed work teams leads to increased engagement by the employee. In general, we expect to see increased responsibility and accountability as the team realizes they are making their own decisions (see Figure 5.3).

5.5 Use of Product Backlog

In our approach to using the scrum technique, we derive the product backlog from a work breakdown structure. We don't necessarily have to use work breakdown structure—it is just a convenient way to merge a tool we have used for years with the

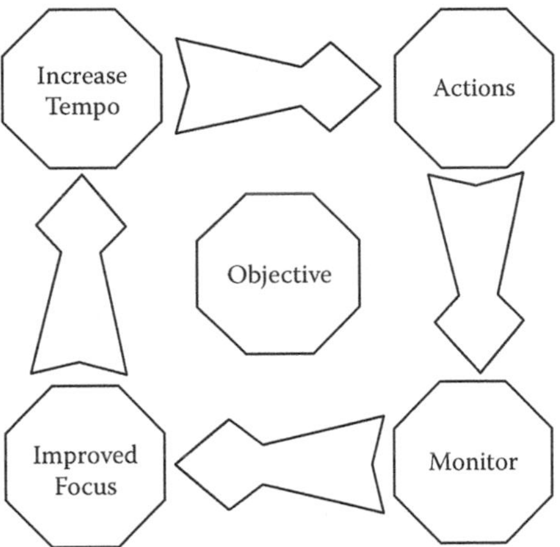

Figure 5.2 Team performance.

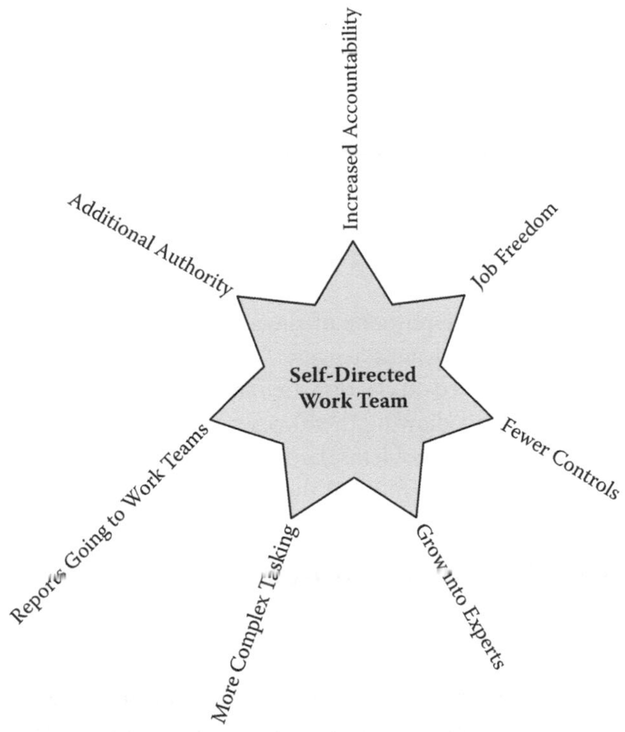

Figure 5.3 Self-directed teams.

newer tool of the scrum. In general, the product backlog functions as a parking lot that allows forecasted atoms that will be assigned to individual sprints. Consequently, the product backlog can be as large as we allow it to be. As a product backlog becomes very large, it can become unmanageable. We see no reason why the product backlog cannot be broken down into sections related to function or possibly synchronized with a more traditional project management technique such as the waterfall or the military systems engineering approach.

One way to maintain a product backlog is to use a simple spreadsheet. Unfortunately, spreadsheets do not provide the level of tools that we really need in order to manage the backlog as it becomes unmanageable. For that purpose, we recommend the use of the database; for example, we could use a simple personal database such as Microsoft Access or we could use a more powerful database like Oracle or MySQL. Either way, we will need fields for such items as the following:

- Status
- Necessary completion date ("drop dead" date)
- Assigned person
- Start date
- Comments
- Hours needed to complete

We could take the database concept as far as we want to go; for example, we could develop a goal of our graphics from the database software itself. The most common graphics tool when using the scrum approach is the burndown chart. Sometimes, generating these charts can be truly tedious. We would want to build in some kind of macro into our database so that we could generate these charts very quickly as well as permit team members' input.

The most easily adoptable portions of the scrum are those parts that have the biggest positive impact on the team's delivery. We use the tools to help keep people in our line organization focused on clearly articulated and measurable objectives. We get more out of the team by allowing them to set their own direction and tapping into their creativity to solve the problems that are at hand. We rely less on regimented processes and more on the adaptability of these creative people.

5.6 Use of Sprint Retrospective

The purpose of the sprint retrospective is to spend some time looking at what we did well and what we would like to improve from the most recent sprint. The retrospective allows time for team learning to occur. Furthermore, the team can voice their suggestions for improvement. If we use this tool, the scrum approach would generally seem like a relatively democratic process and the team members will have a higher sense of ownership in the results. Figure 5.4 shows the content of the team retrospective portion of the sprint meeting.

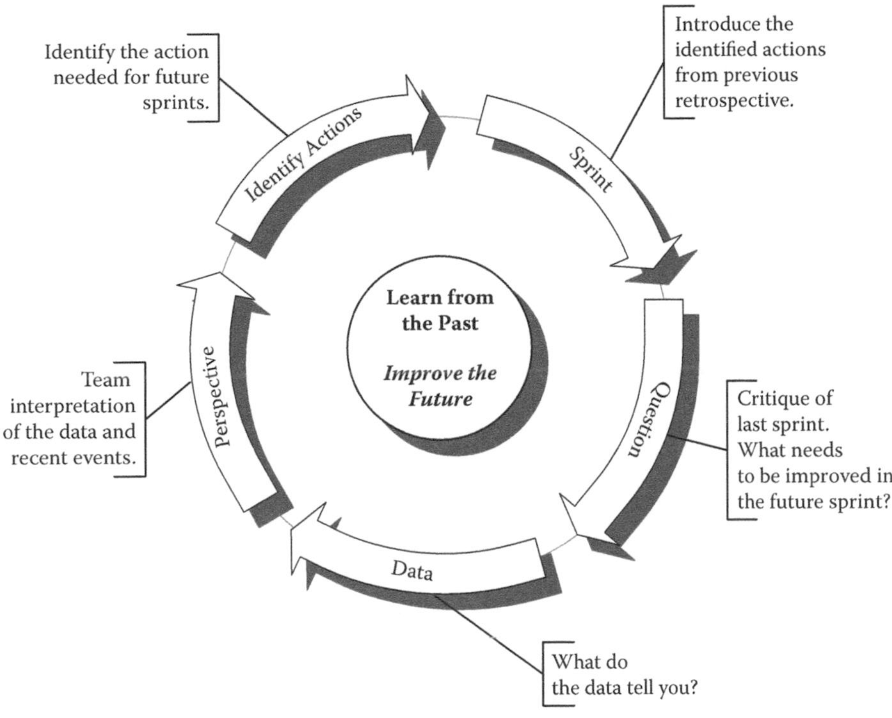
Identify the action needed for future sprints.
Introduce the identified actions from previous retrospective.
Identify Actions
Sprint
Learn from the Past
Improve the Future
Perspective
Question
Team interpretation of the data and recent events.
Critique of last sprint. What needs to be improved in the future sprint?
Data
What do the data tell you?

Figure 5.4 Retrospective.

Because team learning should occur as part of the retrospective, the corrective actions that arise from these discussions should be very real. Here we have a fast-paced chance to perform real process improvement—a chance we should never let pass by for the *sake of expediency.*

Notes

1. Kenneth Blanchard and Robert Lorber, *Putting the One Minute Manager to Work,* (New York, NY: Berkley Books 1984), 58
2. Ken Schwaber, *The Enterprise and Scrum,* (Redmond, WA: Microsoft Press, 2007), 7
3. Timothy Ferris, *The 4-Hour Workweek,* (New York, NY: Crown Publishers, 2007), 133

Chapter 6

Scrum and the Waterfall Method

6.1 The Waterfall Method

The waterfall method or approach is one of the most famous project management models in existence. At its simplest, the implication is that tasks appear and are completed linearly. In a sense, this simplistic representation of the waterfall approach is an aspect of the naive "why can't they get it right the first time" school of management. Another by-product of the simplistic waterfall approach is the burden placed on project management:

- Schedule/timelines that stretch out for months or years and imply substantial prescience
- Resources available and predictable for the duration of the project
- Quality systems in place
- Team players understand their roles

The simplistic model of the waterfall approach has pretty much drawn fire since people first discussed it (see Figure 6.1). It is easy to see why—it is simply unrealistic.

A more sophisticated version of the waterfall approach uses a model with loop backs for the cases where a stage gate in the model cannot be passed and the team must cycle through that phase again. This version of the waterfall approach is more realistic than the simplistic model but it still has flaws; for example:

- The long-term prescient schedule is still part of the system, although it may be perturbed by unplanned phase iterations.
- Resources must be available potentially for even longer duration than expected in the simplistic model.
- All participants still need to know their roles.

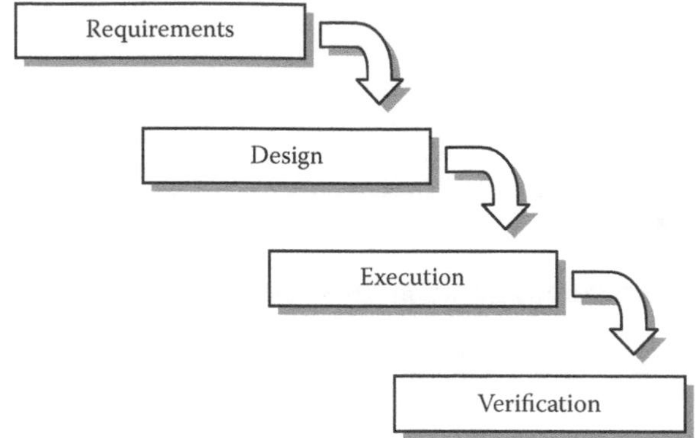

Figure 6.1 Waterfall.

6.1.1 Benefits of the Waterfall Method

Probably the greatest single benefit of the waterfall method is that it is easy to understand. Unfortunately, understanding doesn't always lend itself to ease of implementation. However, the models are so compelling, nearly every staged-gate approach is a variant on the waterfall approach. The automotive-oriented Advanced Product Quality Planning (APQP) approach recommends some level of concurrent engineering but, at heart, it is really a multiply-threaded waterfall philosophy.

6.1.2 Defects of the Waterfall Method

The waterfall method is an example of what we call "crystalline" project management. The plan is rigid and team learning and investigating how to make the product is not built into the system. Often, we over-optimistically project plans where the uncertainties will be addressed when we awaken to them, often too late. Additionally, if the delivery date is years out, we see project managers trying to forecast task completions when they have no way of knowing if their prognostications stand a chance of completion. The unrealistic planning horizon provides no benefits to supplier or customer and may lead to customer frustration and lost business.

6.1.3 Application of Scrum to the Waterfall Method

We see no reason why the enhanced tempo of the scrum approach cannot be applied to the waterfall method. In fact, if we were to look more closely at the scrum approach, we would see that it is really a waterfall method with extremely short durations, sometimes as short as a single day. While the forecasting difficulties of the waterfall approach will still apply over the long duration, the scrum approach provides a sane method for controlling risk, schedule, and budget. By enhancing the tempo, the scrum approach enhances the probability that the waterfall method may actually function as desired.

Before we apply scrum to the waterfall method, we should establish the scrum duration. Most commonly, we see fortnight schedules and month schedules. As we now know, we call these schedules "sprints." The sprint method provides us with a short enough duration–that is to say a planning horizon—that our forecasting accuracy has much lower risk. Once we have established the sprint duration, we can build these periods into a waterfall approach. Other parts of the enterprise may not be using the scrum approach—they may be more comfortable with the waterfall method. By mixing the two models, we allow ourselves the best of both worlds while meeting corporate expectations. Since scrum reporting occurs more frequently than what is typical with the waterfall approach, we lose nothing in our reporting capability. We lose nothing in terms of quality because we have been holding daily scrum meetings and assessing our quality as we proceed through the project. Even better, the budget remains completely under control, thanks to the daily review.

6.1.3.1 Benefits of Applying Scrum

We have noted several times the increased tempo expected when switching to the scrum approach. Our experience suggests that this is one of the greatest benefits to be achieved by using this agile method regardless of the style of project management. The reduced risk caused by the frequent meetings, including the sprint meeting at the end of the period, also provides a salutary effect. Planning and forecasting never exceed a planning horizon that can be managed by the team.

We have also seen improved interplay among team members. In general, no one is allowed to be absent from a scrum meeting. All team members listen to all other team members when answering the three questions. Any break in the time-box must have the acquiescence of all team members in order to occur. In that manner, team members are less resentful of the meetings, and improved communication occurs because everybody hears everybody else on a daily basis. Furthermore, all team members will attend the review and sprint planning meeting, which likewise has a positive effect on communications.

6.1.3.2 Defects of Applying Scrum

We may sound like we are extremely enthusiastic about the application of scrum in a variety of project management and line management projects; however, we have found some detriments to using the scrum approach, particularly when it is applied indiscriminately. One of the defects lies in the mismatch in a given project between a group that applies the scrum method and another team that uses a relatively mundane waterfall approach. In that situation, the waterfall team may not understand what the scrum team is trying to do. The only saving grace when this occurs, particularly when delivering software, is that the goal is to always have a releasable product at the end of each sprint session.

We have seen some cases of mismatch where the mismatch was sufficiently poor that the waterfall team felt a sense of betrayal because the scrum team was not delivering as expected. The responsibility for a situation like this most likely falls on the shoulders of the project manager, who should have communicated the kind of models being used to move the project forward.

When using multiple modalities to arrive at a project goal, the project manager must set up the rules of engagement at the beginning of the project. It is necessary to communicate the means by which progress will be measured and to secure intercommunication among the various teams. Any approach or tool that improves communication among these various teams is a major plus. We suggest that all teams should gather at the major milestones developed for the waterfall approach. That means the scrum teams attend the same reviews as the waterfall teams do. It is not the case that waterfall teams need to attend the daily scrum meetings ever. However, the waterfall teams might give consideration to attending the sprint reviews in planning meetings.

6.1.4 When Not to Use Scrum

Given our enthusiasm for the scrum approach, it might seem odd when we suggest that there may be occasions when the scrum approach is not the best idea. In our experience, the scrum approach takes at least as much if not more discipline than the typical waterfall approach. If the team is not ready for daily scrum meetings, burndown charts, and sprint reviews in planning meetings, then they should not even consider the idea of implementing the scrum approach.

In some corporations, the formal project model may be the waterfall approach. In cases like these, the only way scrum would be implemented would be in the form of an underground movement. That means the practitioners may be taking their jobs in their hands and risking the loss of employment. Another similar example of this situation occurs in product development organizations that have defined the process using a quality standard, a well-defined government approach, or some other highly regulated industry.

6.1.5 When to Use Scrum

We suggest using scrum in relatively small organizations that are already known for their flexibility and tolerance for new ideas. If scrum is going to be implemented in an organization that has not previously used it, then we must use some kind of pilot model so that we can demonstrate to upper management that the risk is minimal. Obviously, organizations that are already using scrum have nothing to worry about other than perhaps proliferating the approach to other parts of the enterprise.

6.2 Managing Conflicts

Conflicts may arise because some team members or managers may consider scrum to be a bearer of false achievement. In that case, we expect to see resistance, if not sabotage, to the scrum teams. As with most initiatives in an enterprise, it is wise to secure buy-in with significant decision-makers such as upper-level managers. Such an endorsement may deflate much of the conflict that can occur, particularly when the new method is deployed. Another alternative would be to use an approach where it is likely that the method will succeed; that is to say, we show the rest of the enterprise that the method will indeed work. This approach is very similar to that used when deploying Six Sigma throughout an enterprise. Hence, a dose of politicking with upper-level management and a wise choice of projects should minimize the initial level of complaints expected from late adopters.

6.3 Managing Risks

Throughout this book, we have indicated that risk management is enhanced, primarily due to the short planning horizon. We suggest with the waterfall method that a concatenation of small risk management sequences will most likely improve any risk management we would expect to find in a waterfall-scrum hybrid. Typical waterfall risk management includes risk identification, risk elimination, and risk mitigation (for those cases where we cannot eliminate the risk). The same rules apply to scrum but for much shorter durations and with an increased chance for success.

6.4 System Development with Scrum and Waterfall Combined

Our previous discussions in this chapter indicate little reason why a scrum-waterfall hybrid shouldn't be successful. Good communication, frequent team meetings, and knowledgable project management should lead to a successful project conclusion. It may turn out that the most difficult part of a scrum deployment in a waterfall organization will lie with convincing the diehards that such an apparently loose method can deliver anything at all; however, the "looseness" is nothing but illusion. If anything, the scrum approach is more rigorous and less prone to self-lying than any other project management methodology. The scrum approach contains everything the waterfall approach has but in much shorter durations. We again make the analogy to the heart of lean manufacturing—rapid replenishment. The increase in tempo makes the difference.

6.4.1 Pre-Deployment

We recommend that pre-deployment be largely an information dissemination exercise. In short, we will supply the entire project staff with documentation, either paper or electronic, that explains the history and philosophy behind the scrum approach. If we have introduced scrum earlier, we can discuss how successful the program was and also any difficulties encountered during the project. Scrum teams that are newly formed and have never actually practiced will need training before the project starts. The training difficulties we expect to see are similar to those we have seen with Six Sigma projects and lean initiatives.

The following list indicates what the training plan for the initial implementation of scrum would look like. Please note that this plan is a recommendation; obviously, each organization will tailor this plan to their specific needs.

- Introduction to scrum
- Genesis of scrum in agile development
- Agile principles
  - Complex adaptive systems
  - Adaptive management
  - High-intensity management
- Roles
  - Scrum Master
  - Product owner
  - Team member
  - Stakeholders
  - Managers
- Meetings
  - Daily scrum
  - Sprint planning
  - Sprint review
  - Sprint retrospective
- Documentation
  - Sprint backlog
  - Product backlog
  - Burndown chart
- Overall project plan
  - Project schedule
  - Project reviews
  - Project milestones

Also during pre-deployment, we suggest that the project management team or group choose a project for the scrum implementation that is likely to be successful. This approach allows the scrum team to metaphorically get their feet wet and simultaneously reduce the risk of implementing a new modality in the enterprise. As with any new technique, the people involved will not quite understand what is expected of them regardless of the amount of communication and training implemented before the project actually starts. In fact, some late adopters will most likely do this new scrum approach as yet another flavor of the month foisted on them by a management organization that never seems to understand their specific problems. So the order of the day is to keep the project relatively simple and straightforward.

6.4.2 Initial Deployment

When scrum is first deployed, the first few sprints will be primarily planning activities. The rules of engagement will be worked out, the duration of the sprint will be determined, and all the critical tests will be defined, including reporting, both what and to whom. If the scrum teams do not spend any time on this early work, they will end up doing it later on, which is likely to reduce performance. The point is to provide training that includes a concise set of basic procedures that define the required scrum activities. The procedures provide structure for the initial deployment. The scrum deployment team may decide to modify the procedures later as the teams learn how to function with each other; however, the basics of product and sprint backlogs, daily scrum meetings, and burndown charts should remain or we are not really practicing scrum.

6.4.3 Follow-Up Deployment

Once we have implemented the scrum approach for a while, perhaps a month or two, we suggest it would be wise to hold an internal review simply to see how we are doing with this new approach. We recommend that waterfall team members participate in the reviews as scrum team members. The goal in this meeting will lie in the quality of the constructive criticism applied by all participants. The interaction among team members should be respectful, open-minded, yet critical. We would expect to see a substantial amount of dialectical interaction when all team members have a reasonable amount of self-esteem. What we want to avoid during this particular session is any kind of elitism displayed by either group of teams. The following example agenda shows one approach that could be used during this meeting to structure meeting actions and results:

- Overall project
  - Project schedule review
  - Project budget review
  - Known quality issues
  - Milestones accomplished
  - Traditional reviews completed
  - Earned value metrics
  - Next meeting
  - Current anticipated completion date
- Waterfall teams
  - In-process reviews
  - Variance against overall project metrics
  - Verification and validation

- Scrum teams
  - Sprint reviews
  - Variance against overall project metrics
  - Verification and validation

6.4.4 The "Big" Team Meeting

The big team meeting occurs sometime during the middle of the project. This meeting is not a formal milestone in the sense that it is directly related to the project. It is another occasion for all teams to mingle and for the project manager to understand the status of all segments of the project. By using the big team meeting, we can avoid the situation where we have an endgame mismatch between the scrum teams and waterfall teams or scrum teams and scrum teams. The following list shows what an agenda for such a meeting could look like:

- Overall project
  - Project schedule review
  - Project budget review
  - Known quality issues
  - Milestones accomplished
  - Traditional reviews completed
  - Earned value metrics
  - Current anticipated completion date
- Waterfall teams
  - In-process reviews (if these exist—they should!)
  - Variance against overall project metrics
  - Verification and validation results
- Scrum teams
  - Sprint reviews
  - Variance against overall project metrics
  - Verification and validation results
- Synchronization
  - Locate sprint team results against overall plan
  - Locate waterfall team results against overall plan
  - Determine the gap among or between the teams
  - Produce a sprint document to eliminate the gap
  - Verify gap removed on completion of sprint

6.4.5 Communications Practices

A significant amount of communication is already built into the scrum approach; for example, we know the scrum team will meet on a daily basis. If we have the scrum of scrums, we still expect each individual team to meet on a daily basis and we also expect the team leaders to meet with the next level up on a daily basis as well. We may, however, run into difficulties with the waterfall group—they may not be meeting as frequently as the scrum teams meet. In most of the projects we have witnessed, waterfall teams meet approximately once a week, usually for one hour to 90 minutes. Sometimes, participants may feel more is lost during these meetings than is gained since the length of these meetings accommodates joke-making, pontificating, and personal agendas.

What we call the big meeting can help with intercommunication issues among scrum and waterfall teams. What it cannot do, however, is eliminate communications issues for teams that don't have scrum meetings built into their process. If we move the waterfall teams toward the scrum meetings, then they become *de facto* scrum teams. Given our enthusiasm for the scrum approach, we don't see this as a particularly evil event. On the other hand, if the enterprise has a formal process that requires the existence of the waterfall teams, we may run into resistance from both management and waterfall-style gatekeepers.

6.4.6 Sprints versus Milestones

Part of the purpose of the big team meeting that we have previously discussed is to align sprint activities with the formal milestones that belong to the waterfall approach. We see no reason why it should be difficult to synchronize a sequence of sprints with the previously defined milestones of the project. In fact, the milestones themselves provide yet another opportunity for both the scrum and the waterfall teams to mingle and communicate. Furthermore, milestones or gates closed usually have upper-level managers and attendants, so these milestones can also function as kill points. In most formal processes that we have seen, it takes an executive level decision in order to kill or terminate an existing project (see Figure 6.2).

In spite of our ominous heading for this section, we believe the sprints and milestones are completely compatible. Obviously, a modicum of planning will help synchronize these different approaches. In general, we consider the synchronization to be a simple issue with project timing. The issue is simple because the scrum approach iterates so often that we can match up any other milestones or reviews with the scrum activities.

6.4.7 What About Verification and Validation?

Observant readers may wonder about what kind of testing we would expect to see in a scrum-waterfall hybrid. If we are talking about software testing (verification and validation), then testing is built into the scrum process. However, we may have limitations during the development of product hardware that can cause timing issues between the scrum and waterfall teams. We recommend an approach similar to that used by the United States Department of Defense—the implementation of a test and evaluation master plan (TEMP). We can use the TEMP to drive the concentric ring system we described earlier, with each verification/validation activity following each

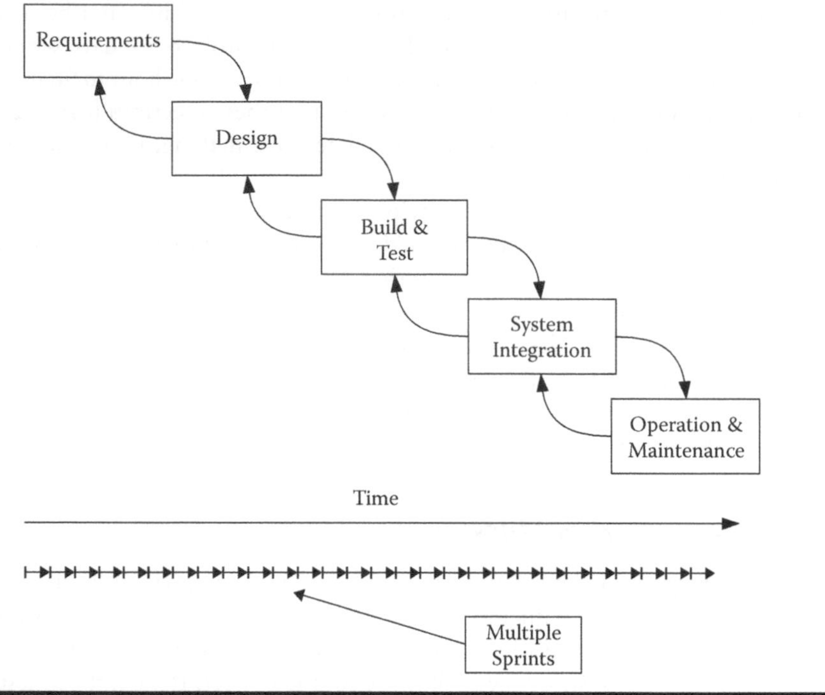

Figure 6.2 Scrum and waterfall projects to develop a system.

ring (release). If the TEMP is little more than a long-range waterfall for testing, we can expect the same difficulties we have seen in the waterfall method for the entire project: schedule and budget slippage and verification/validation crunched at the end of the project. If the TEMP is criterion-based, then we can expect verification and validation to occur at the proper moments from the point of view of meeting the criteria. In order to use a criterion-based approach, the project manager must understand all of the dependencies that go into various releases of the hardware. Without this level of understanding, it is less likely that testing will occur synchronously with hardware development. Figure 6.3 shows how the verification phase gets crunched at the end of the process.

Even when we use a criterion-based system, waterfall practitioners tend to construct project schedules with minimal releases of testable products. Consequently, even if we are using a waterfall-scrum hybrid, the waterfall orientation may lead us into a situation where no hardware and no software are available for verification and validation until the usual crunch period.

The scrum teams will generally have something like a test and evaluation master plan built in to their product backlogs. Consequently, the risk of not testing is effectively nonexistent in the scrum approach, particularly given the fact that the goal of the scrum team is to always have some kind of deliverable product.

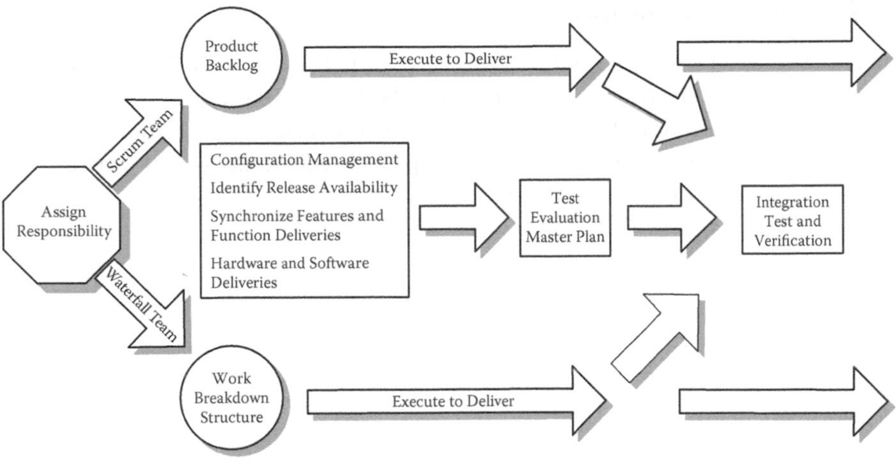

Figure 6.3 Scrum and waterfall and verification.

6.4.8 Bringing the Project to a Close

Just as an airplane approaches the airport runway, the endgame of the project may have its difficulties, not the least of which is synchronizing the diverse threads that the various teams are executing to terminate in an orderly manner. At this point, the experience or wisdom of a really good project manager will most likely be essential to bring the project to a successful terminus. It is possible that the multiple teams may no longer be well-synchronized. If that is the case, the project manager should have another big team meeting so that all the teams can communicate their project status in front of all the other teams and, as a group, they can arrive at a consensus as to how the project will end. This approach does not mean the project manager abdicates responsibility but, rather, allows the participants to own their share of the project endgame.

6.4.9 Challenges

The rate of delivery of the constituent components for a system is the chief challenge during any coordination activity. The result of these mismatches is that the delivery of the system will be a spasmodic process. We should be using a configuration management system to help with synchronization of the delivered pieces, allowing us to adapt to the actual delivery. This situation is true whether the scrum functional content is different than expected or the waterfall organization is the part of the organization delivering unexpected functionality. Either way, we are looking at a potential fiasco.

6.4.10 Risk Mitigation

The easiest way to mitigate the risk with a waterfall-scrum hybrid is to eliminate the symmetrical control setup we have described and make the waterfall rhythm subservient to the scrum rhythm. If we use a musical analogy, the scrum teams will be playing at 4/4 time, but the waterfall groups will synchronize on the syncopation notes, say every second or fourth note.

Chapter 7

Scrum and Education

7.1 Do Scrum and Education Systems Fit?

As we already know, the original scrum approach came from the world of agile software development. It may seem somewhat bizarre to consider using scrum in the best educational system, particularly in the United States. We see no reason why this cannot be the case and we have proposed this approach to at least one major school district. Figure 7.1 shows how we can align a single sprint with the existing structure of school timelines in the United States. Our semester has a six-week period at the beginning, which can have two three-week sprints which include five working days for each week or fifteen days for the sprint.

7.2 What Scrum Can Do for the Educational System

Although school systems are nearly always composed of certified professionals, they often become insular societies. The inhabitants of this society will know a whole lot about their specific areas, but often have not been exposed to industrial practices or federal government practices. Because educational systems are intrinsically bureaucratic systems, they become prone to significant inefficiencies when it comes to tasks not related directly to education. The scrum team approach can improve the tempo of performance, as well as provide ample documentation for appropriate levels of governance by the local school boards, not to mention the state agencies. We will provide some examples where we feel the scrum approach will dramatically accelerate accomplishment in certain departments.

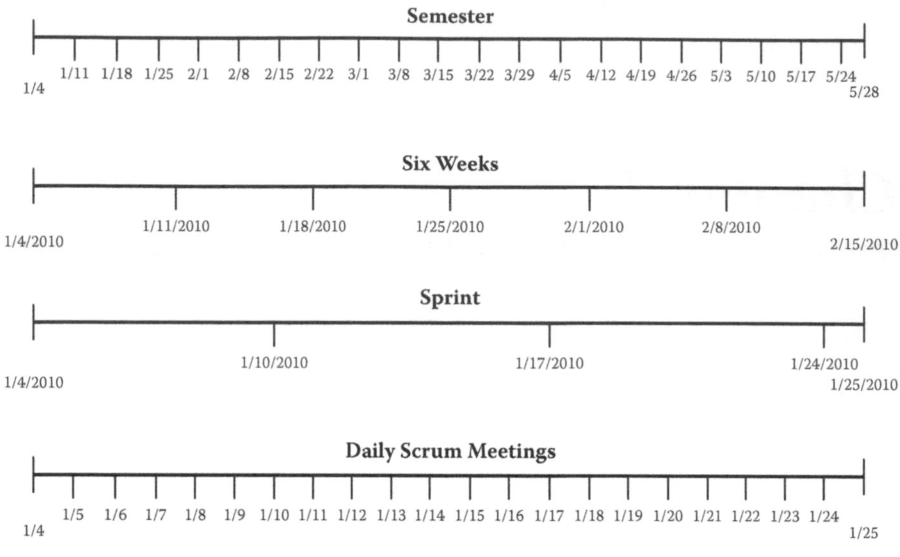

Figure 7.1 Scrum and education.

7.3 Deployment of Scrum in a School

We see no reason why the scrum approach cannot be used in teaching departments. Many of these departments already have daily meetings—the scrum approach supplies a high-intensity structure to what already exists. The long planning horizon often used with product backlogs can be helpful in annual planning or multi-annual planning. Multiple sprints bring the activities to reality and the sprint reviews allow for minor adjustments to improve performance. School departments, particularly in educational subjects, already do substantial planning so adding a high-intensity approach, the short meetings, and a built-in documentation technique for progress should be almost no burden for these already often overburdened professionals.

7.4 Deployment of Scrum in Administrative Offices

We see even stronger opportunities for improvement when scrum is applied in administrative offices. The very short meetings typical of scrum should improve performance from the very start. The product backlog provides an opportunity for campus improvement plans as well as routine tasks. We would also expect to see substantial use of scrum and scrum teams for extracurricular activities.

In addition to having both educational and administrative departments use scrum, we can also teach the approach to students. Modern education strongly supports the idea during group work, especially given the fact that most students will grow into adults who at one time or another will work on teams. Why not teach them this high-intensity approach during their pre-college education?

7.5 Using Scrum with Educational Support Groups

7.5.1 Nutrition

Most schools in the United States provide some level of nutritional support for the students; in some cases, these meals are the best meals that impoverished students will eat during their week. The improved planning and high-cadence execution of the scrum approach can only improve what already occurs in nutritional departments across the United States. Menus, ingredients, and new techniques can be deployed with each sprint.

7.5.2 Busing

Providing transportation to move students from home to school and back again is a huge industry within the educational system. Once again, the scrum approach can provide daily updates, accountability, and improve performance. The educational system might consider using a scrum team to come up with bus route optimization approaches that could potentially save any given school district millions of dollars.

The daily reporting also helps see to the maintenance of the bus fleet when needed. Of course, the school system will have some kind of preventive maintenance plan, but the daily reporting provides evidence of problems that occur in spite of preventive maintenance. In fact, the daily scrum meeting can behave a little bit like a vehicle sensor and thus provide us with an element of predictive maintenance.

7.5.3 Building Maintenance

In some ways, building maintenance is very similar to vehicle maintenance. Nearly every school district will have a plan for inspection and repair of buildings and physical plants. The daily scrum meeting allows management to become aware of maintenance issues as they arise. One example of a major maintenance issue is the presence of mold and mildew in buildings that are either located in the human environment or buildings that use evaporative cooling. If the colonies of mold can be eradicated when they are relatively limited in size, the damage to the building and health issues for students should be minimal. Unfortunately, notification of the presence of mold is not often reported. The plan to deal with mold and mildew should include preventive maintenance, frequent auditing, and some investment in time during the daily scrum meeting.

7.5.4 Safety

Once we detect a safety issue, it will assume the highest priority. The daily scrum meeting, as usual, is one way to ensure that progress occurs against priority issues. Safety issues should rise to the top of product backlogs and sprint backlogs. There can be no excuse for putting our children and our employees at risk because nobody was checking on the system.

Chapter 8

Scrum and Six Sigma

The scrum approach is a wonderful tool to use with any kind of Six Sigma project. Scrum began with software projects and the Six Sigma methodology is also strongly based on the use of projects. Wedding the two approaches should be effortless because their project-oriented methods are related.

8.1 Six Sigma Roles

In traditional Six Sigma, several roles are defined. For example, the role of Champion serves to guide the Black Belt or the Green Belt and is generally at the executive level so they can remove obstacles to progress. The project will typically be executed by a Black Belt or Green Belt—both of whom may have teams. Any one of these roles can serve as a Scrum Master so long as it makes sense. We suggest that an obvious choice for Scrum Master is the Champion if they have available time for very short, daily scrum meetings with their various Six Sigma belt teams. Furthermore, if the Black Belt or the Green Belt practitioner is working with a team, then it makes sense for them to use the daily scrum meeting, the sprints, and the burndown charts to track the progress of their Six Sigma project.

8.2 Typical Six Sigma Deployment

In general, a Six Sigma deployment has a significant investment in training: Champions, Master Black Belts, Black Belts, Green Belts, and any other designation deemed necessary to the success of the deployment. Regardless, all roles must be trained in such Six Sigma concepts as the following:

- Recognition
- Define
- Measure

- Analyze
- Improve
- Control
- Standardize

For each of the concepts listed, we need to develop a training program that balances common sense with the necessary statistical background to actualize the project. The statistics used in Six Sigma run the gamut from simple statistical tests such as the T-test all the way to much more sophisticated analyses such as multivariate regression analysis and designed experiments.

8.3 Six Sigma Deployment with Scrum

We can certainly use the scrum approach during the deployment process. In fact, we know that the scrum approach will actually accelerate the tempo of the deployment while providing improved control and reduced risk. The team tasked with the responsibility of the deployment should resort to the literature to build a product backlog for the deployment. We can do this using either the work breakdown structure approach or a "canned" approach that we distill from the literature. Once we have a reasonably complete product backlog, we can then convert that backlog into a collection of sprint backlogs and, in turn, convert what is in the sprint backlogs into daily tasks for individuals. If we are not using full time Black Belts or Green Belts, we can use the power of our planning and the atomic breakdown of testing to accomplish at least a small amount every day—something we call "the power of the routine task." We have used the power of the routine task many times to steal 15 to 20 minutes a day from all of our other responsibilities so that we keep the project moving forward. When we finish our sprint, if our planning has been well considered, we might be a little surprised at how much we've accomplished with the power of the routine task. In the case where we are conducting a hostile deployment—that is to say, under the radar of management—the power of the routine task is probably the only way to get the job done without attracting attention. Figure 8.1 shows the five standard steps to a Six Sigma project with the daily scrum meetings represented as little arrow circles and the end of phase as scrum meetings.

No matter what the preliminary details are, we will still conduct all appropriate meetings that are a part of the scrum approach. The daily scrum meeting may actually be performed using something we call virtual scrum. Virtual scrum occurs when we use an e-mail that answers the three questions, because if we are only allocating twenty minutes a day to our "routine task," we may not have a lot to report. Please note we also use the virtual scrum ideas through e-mail on occasions when some members of the team are off-site and we don't have access to video conferencing.

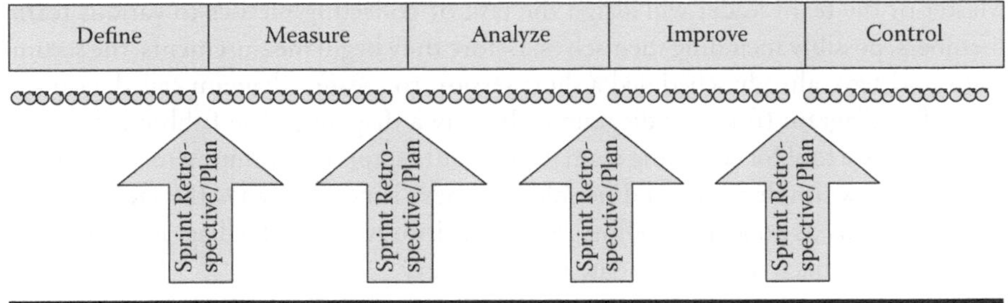

Figure 8.1 Six Sigma and scrum.

8.4 Six Sigma Phases

8.4.1 Recognize

The *recognize* phase in a Six Sigma project is not always a formal act of a team. In fact, recognition may arise more as a surprise or a realization than anything else. The recognize phase is really more of a call to action or a realization of corporate pain than an activity that has a specific process for execution.

8.4.2 Define

The *define* phase occurs once we decide to formalize a project. During this time, we put together a team and we can begin using the scrum approach. If we were using project management terminology, the fine would probably be called scope management. Basically, we are trying to decide what the problem really is and also what it really is not. If we cannot define the problem, we are most likely not going to know the direction we are heading. Hence, this particular phase of any project may be one of the most important if not the most important.

We may also wish to consider introducing formalisms such as a project charter. With Six Sigma, this particular artifact may not be necessary in that we have already defined our project, at least in terms of activities, by using the product backlog. We will refine the product backlog during the define phase; indeed, we will be revising or adding to the product backlog through the entire project. We update our define scope because we are learning about our project as we work our way through the steps. By no means is the Define, Measure, Analyze, Improve, and Control approach carved into stone.

8.4.3 Measure

During the *measure* phase, we take the scope we have defined and we decide which metrics we will apply to that scope. We should baseline the existing situation before we attempt any analyses or improvements—this step provides us with the information we need in order to determine if an improvement really did change things for the better. The scrum approach fits in well with the measure phase. Basically, the Scrum

Master or the team leader will assign the task of collecting metrics to various team members, possibly including themselves. Before they begin measurements, the scrum team may have already scheduled a short session to create a diagram called a cause-and-effect diagram (fishbone diagram or Ishikawa diagram). The fishbone diagram is a qualitative tool for collecting team ideas about factors contributing to the defined problem. It is simple to use and its sole weakness is nearly always the fact that the diagram is only as good as the effort that is put into it. Once the diagram exists, the team can refer back to it and update it as necessary.

The *measure* phase can be extremely labor-intensive. If the factors that produce the undesired response are not well known, we will have to collect enough data to perform an analysis that will help us decide which factors are significant to the response (a response is the result of applying stimuli; we can have more than one response). These kinds of activities must all be captured in the product backlog and parceled out into the sprint backlogs. We often use Excel spreadsheets with multiple columns where each row signifies the calendar day. We lay out the product backlog in priority order by day.

8.4.4 Analyze

The *analyze* phase is the duration in which our scrum team will take the data they have captured during the major phase and begin to mine it for revelations. It is during the analyze phase that the scrum team will often make use of substantial statistical tools. Sometimes simple Pareto charts are adequate to direct the team toward the solution. The scrum team needs to be sufficiently well-trained so that they know which tools to use and how to use them.

We will most likely need a team member with a strong background in statistics during the analyze phase. Typical Six Sigma projects often analyze the data for descriptive statistics such as mean and variance at a minimum. More exotic analyses may examine the data for goodness-of-fit to non-normal probability distributions, for time series analyses, and multivariate regression analyses.

8.4.5 Improve

Once we have finished our data collecting and our analyses, our scrum team will begin to formulate a solution to the defined problem. Typical tools used during this *improve* phase include designed experiments, response surface methodologies, regression analyses, and a variety of search algorithms, including the sequential simplex algorithm, particle swarm optimization, and genetic algorithms. Since our scrum team will most likely have already recorded baseline data values, they can record data values from the post-improvement phase to determine if any improvement actually occurred. In some cases, they will use a tool called control charts, which are really a time series with special limits used to determine when statistically significant events have occurred.

8.4.6 Control

Six Sigma practitioners use the *control* phase as a means to make their improvements sustainable. Once the scrum team has put in the effort to analyze data and make improvements, it would seem wise that they spend the time to ensure that the improvements continue and will be used by the rest of the enterprise. Control charts are one of the most important tools during this phase: They visually disclose the difference between random variation and assignable causes. Scrum teams may also opt to use simple run charts or gate charts (a gate chart shows a vertical line for a "clean" date—we should see improvement after the clean date indicating the control is working).

8.4.7 Standardize

Standardize might not be considered a phase by many Six Sigma practitioners; however, it is with standardization that we truly formalize our new improvements and controls and ensure that they become part of the culture of our enterprise. We have seen simple controls degrade with the passage of time simply because the users could no longer remember why the controls were in place. Once the meaning of a control disappears, users will often apply it sporadically if at all—one of the most common areas we see this situation is in manufacturing plants.

If the enterprise already has a quality management system, the process for standardizing improvements should already be documented. This document should occur in the sequence of policy, procedure, work instruction, and records. If the enterprise does not have a quality management system, then it would make sense to emulate the ISO-9000 process or some other similar quality standard.

8.5 Design for Six Sigma (DFSS)

Design for Six Sigma arose because Six Sigma practitioners found their process stifled at roughly five sigma using the define, measure, analyze, improve, and control phases alone. In order to reach Six Sigma, they would have to use some of the methods used in standard Six Sigma and apply them to the design process—that is what DFSS is all about. The scrum team approach is applicable to the ideas of DFSS. Common tools include the quality function deployment, designed experiments, failure mode and effects analyses, and any other tool that will improve the robustness of the final product.

If we are going to use designed experiments during the design of the product and the process, then we need to have a product on which to perform the experiments. Here is the point at which the ability to use simulations becomes incredibly important because we can substitute the simulator for the real product. If we have good simulators we can adjust the factors we want to adjust as many times as we would like and record the response to each adjustment. Good simulators also give us a leg up on the competition. With hardware products, simulators would include SPICE (electrical circuit simulator) for electronics and finite element analysis and computational fluid dynamics for mechanical design. The software engineers might have to write their own simulator.

Chapter 9

Scrum and Systems Engineering Defense-Style

In this chapter, we show how we can merge a military standard and the scrum approach. In many cases, military programs become very large, yet we think there is a place for the scrum approach even in a relatively regulated environment such as a large-scale project or program.

9.1 Systems Engineering Planning Implementation

The military approach is very strong on systems engineering as an alternative to poor project management. Because of that, we are more likely to see the term "systems engineering" rather than the term "project management." In many cases, the concepts are equivalent. One of the strong suits of the military approach lies in the use of substantial planning. We are not contradicting ourselves in the comments we made on the waterfall approach. What we are saying here is that there are some strengths to be gained from a long-term approach to military projects based on the experience of decades. We suggest that a prudent combination of both approaches will lead to a whole that is greater than the sum of its parts.

The management and control of multiple entities, both governmental and civilian, are a hallmark of military programs. Because of the complexity caused by this multiplicity of entities, significant forethought is necessary in order to diminish the probability of a failure. Although we can consider this multiplicity of entities to be analogous to the use of suppliers by a civilian company, we believe there are some strong differences in military and some other governmental programs; for example, in many programs, the final results are often heavily controlled by regulatory requirements. We can expect significant regulatory requirements with programs for the Federal Aviation Administration, the Food and Drug Administration, and any other agency that has a high component of safety as part of its mission. Because of the regulatory requirements, we need to consider the use of an overall system approach as a solution to the mission requirements.

Do not confuse the project schedule or plan with the overall systems engineering approach. The systems engineering approach consists of a holistic view of the overall program. Because the government has decades of experience with military programs—small to the incredibly gigantic—some of the items in the systems engineering standard read almost like a checklist, which keeps us from forgetting items that are ultimately essential to the success of the mission and the program. Furthermore, systems engineering standards generally put much more emphasis on technical performance management, decision support, and sustainable product support. Nearly every major task in the systems engineering realm can benefit from application of the scrum approach; for example, we can have a scrum team develop the supplier comparison study (called a "trade study" in defense argot).

9.2 Systems Engineering Input and Technical Objectives

With large government programs, the input and the requirements will often be generated by the agency itself. In short, the agency will negotiate with and offer contracts to a collection of contracting agencies in order to develop a product or service in fulfillment of the requirements created by the agency itself. Because this approach is typical with government agencies, especially the military, a significant responsibility is placed on the team that develops the requirements because it is the requirements in the related statement of work that will define the final product. With the military, a standard exists for defining performance requirements rather than specifying so much detail that the contractor has no ability to use his own technical knowledge to provide a solution, particularly a cost-effective solution that really meets the needs of the contract. Table 9.1 is a list of standards applicable to specifications.

If we are discussing a large contract, we would expect the traditional systems engineering activities of requirements elicitation and formal document generation

Table 9.1 Specification Standards

Commercial item descriptions	GSA Standardization Manual
Standard performance specifications	MIL-STD-961D
Guide specifications	DoD 4120.3-M
Program-unique specifications	MIL-STD-961D

to apply. During this phase of the program, we would not expect a scrum team to be developing any documentation, verification plans, or any other artifacts related to the program.

9.3 Systems Engineering Process Requirements

9.3.1 Requirements Analysis

As part of the systems engineering process, we would expect to see a substantial amount of time and resources consumed to analyze the existing situation and the desired situation so as to produce a set of requirements. For most government agencies, the format of the requirements will already be defined by a government standard. If the systems engineering function intends to use the scrum approach, it would be well to invite the teams to participate during the later portions of the requirements analysis. The reason we are putting off the action by the scrum teams is because the scrum teams themselves are not a systems engineering function. As we have seen so far in this book, we already know the scrum teams will be well-equipped to deal with detailed issues, but perhaps less well equipped to deal with the overall systems approach.

It is conceivable during the requirements analysis phase of any program that we might use a scrum of scrum approach to manage the development of the requirements document. We are suggesting that extending the scrum approach to this portion of the program may not be the best approach at the time. Requirements analysis is an activity where we are less interested in speeding up the tempo and more interested in completeness.

9.3.2 Functional Analysis of Allocation

Functional analysis of allocation means our systems engineering function will be considering which portions of the requirements will be allocated to what kind of contractor. This kind of activity is extremely specific to systems engineering and has almost nothing to do with the scrum approach. We might view the functional analysis of allocation activity as an anticipatory function rather than an element of the execution phase. Remember that government contracts are often written in terms of millions or billions of dollars and the ultimate allocation of funds and staffing is a significant responsibility. So, once again, we are less interested in picking up the tempo and more interested in equitable distribution of tasks and monies.

9.3.3 Synthesis

Synthesis is a great word for the design activity because it captures the fact that we are producing something that has not existed before. Synthesis has the opposite meaning of "analysis," which is what we already accomplished with trade studies and requirements capture.

9.3.3.1 Design

By the time we begin to design, we already have requirements developed by the systems engineering function during an earlier phase of the program. At this stage in the program, the scrum teams can come to the fore. We see no reason why the scrum approach cannot be another tool in the armamentarium of a government project or program. When we develop software using the scrum approach, we often use an artifact called "stories." We will often see stories written on index cards, on pieces of paper, or stored in databases. Use of these stories on a government program may lead to some issues with standardized requirements or regulatory requirements. Some of the government standards will specify the type of document or artifact that needs to be produced by the team and those will bear no resemblance to stories. We don't think the potential for a non-story requirement is particularly deadly to the scrum approach. The use of stories is an activity that arose out of the extreme programming approach developed during the 1990s. Whether we use the scrum approach during design will be the responsibility of the systems engineering function or of project or program management.

9.3.3.2 Design Verification

Large programs can generate large verification problems, not only during the design activities but also during the qualification trials. The systems engineering function should be amply qualified to make decisions about the resources needed in order to perform design verification. Why is this such a problem? We believe this can become a problem in situations where the financial cost of verification is high. If we are talking about weapon system development, we may even have to locate facilities where the system can be tested without causing damage to the surrounding environment. This level of design verification is not tractable for the scrum teams.

The scrum approach to design verification generally occurs during the very first sprints completed by the scrum teams. The scrum team activities are more likely to be used for development of high-technology items such as software, printed circuit boards, sophisticated electronics, and complex manufacturing processes. That is why we suggest that the development of large-scale design verification is really a responsibility of systems engineering or program management; that is, the issue requires an individual or individuals with a more system-level or global perspective. When customer-proprietary hardware is not available at a supplier site, it becomes necessary to negotiate testing time at the customer site; in short, if we can't do it here, we have to do it there.

9.3.4 Systems Analysis and Control

A collection of activities designed to provide controls (as we call them in the automotive industry) exists to support the systems engineering function. A scrum team can accomplish this objective by analyzing the systems and subsystems using a process failure mode and effects analysis (PFMEA) approach. The use of a scrum team in this application makes a lot of sense because PFMEA development is nearly always team based.

9.3.4.1 Trade-Off Studies

Trade-off studies involve comparisons of contractors, products, components, subsystems, and systems in general. One of the best-known methods of developing a trade-off study is to use an approach called Pugh concept development. The process occurs as follows:

1. Develop a set of—potentially weighted—criteria based on customer's requirements, whether those are wants or needs.
2. Develop a group of design concepts, contractors, products, or other items aimed at satisfying the criteria we developed already.
3. Use as simple a matrix as possible and list criteria on the left and the concepts (products, contractors, etc.) across the top.
4. Select one of the concepts as a baseline, usually an existing product, contractor, or other.
5. Evaluate each concept (column heading) against the datum for each of the criteria (row heading). If an item is better, assign a '+'; if the same, assign a '0'; or if it is worse than the baseline, assign a '–'. If we have a plethora of options we can add '+ +' and '– –' or assign numerical values. Do not make it more complicated as long as the array is working.
6. Record the decisions made by the team on a paper or spreadsheet.
7. For each column, we calculate the number of pluses, minuses, and sames or we can take the sum of the alternate score multiplied by weight of the criterion in much the same way as used during a quality function deployment.
8. Iterate the process of developing concepts.

More complex techniques exist; for example, the analytical hierarchy process. It is not so important what techniques we use, but rather that we achieve an equitable selection in what we are aiming to use. We recommend the Pugh approach because it is easy to use, simple to explain, and reasonably powerful. If the team understands the rationale behind the choices they make, they are more likely to support the choice than when management imposes the decision on them without their input.

9.3.4.2 System/Cost-Effectiveness Analysis

The system and cost-effectiveness analysis on a large project for the government will most likely be performed by a function dedicated to financial analysis; for example, the accounting department. Because budget and schedule reporting are central to the government approach, especially on military projects, we do not expect scrum teams to participate in this particular activity. That does not mean that an accounting department cannot use some kind of scrum approach for their own

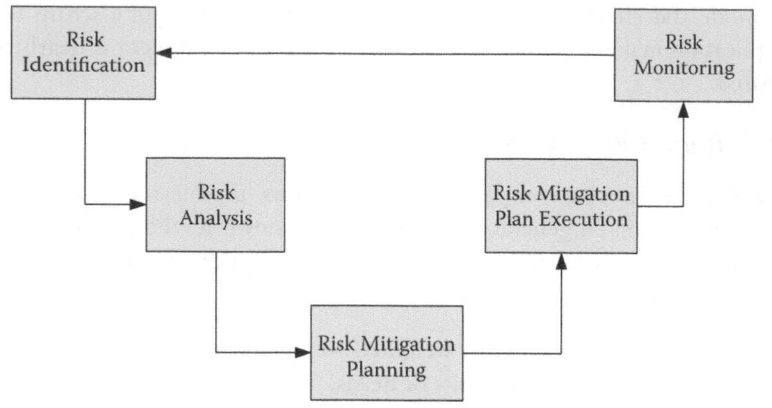

Figure 9.1 DoD and risk.

internal projects—instead, the regulatory requirements of a government project really expect a dedicated department. In general, the contract or contracts will spell out the reporting formats, the reporting intervals, and the functions that need to submit these cost status/cost reporting documents.

9.3.4.3 Risk Management

The plan for managing risk is an integral part of any government contract, regardless of the agency involved (see Figure 9.1). We have discussed risk management in other parts of this book and those rules will apply in this section as well. However, on large programs, a more formal level of documentation will be necessary to meet standardized requirements. In other words, the format and reporting frequency for risk management will already be spelled out in the contract documents. It is possible that the scrum teams will participate in failure mode and effects analyses. A failure mode and effects analysis is a tool for anticipating failures and managing them before they occur. The failure mode and effects analysis is not specifically a scrum-based activity, but we see no good reason why the scrum teams should not perform this analysis.

9.3.4.4 Configuration Management

Configuration management is a requirement for any project (see Figure 9.2). Configuration management per se is not a scrum activity—it is a repeated action performed by members of scrum teams to protect the intellectual property of the enterprise. That means the scrum teams, the conventional teams, and any other contractor or developer will participate in configuration identification, configuration control, configuration status accounting, and configuration auditing. Note that a physical configuration audit is a typical part of a government contract and will involve verifying that the required documentation has been produced by all teams—including

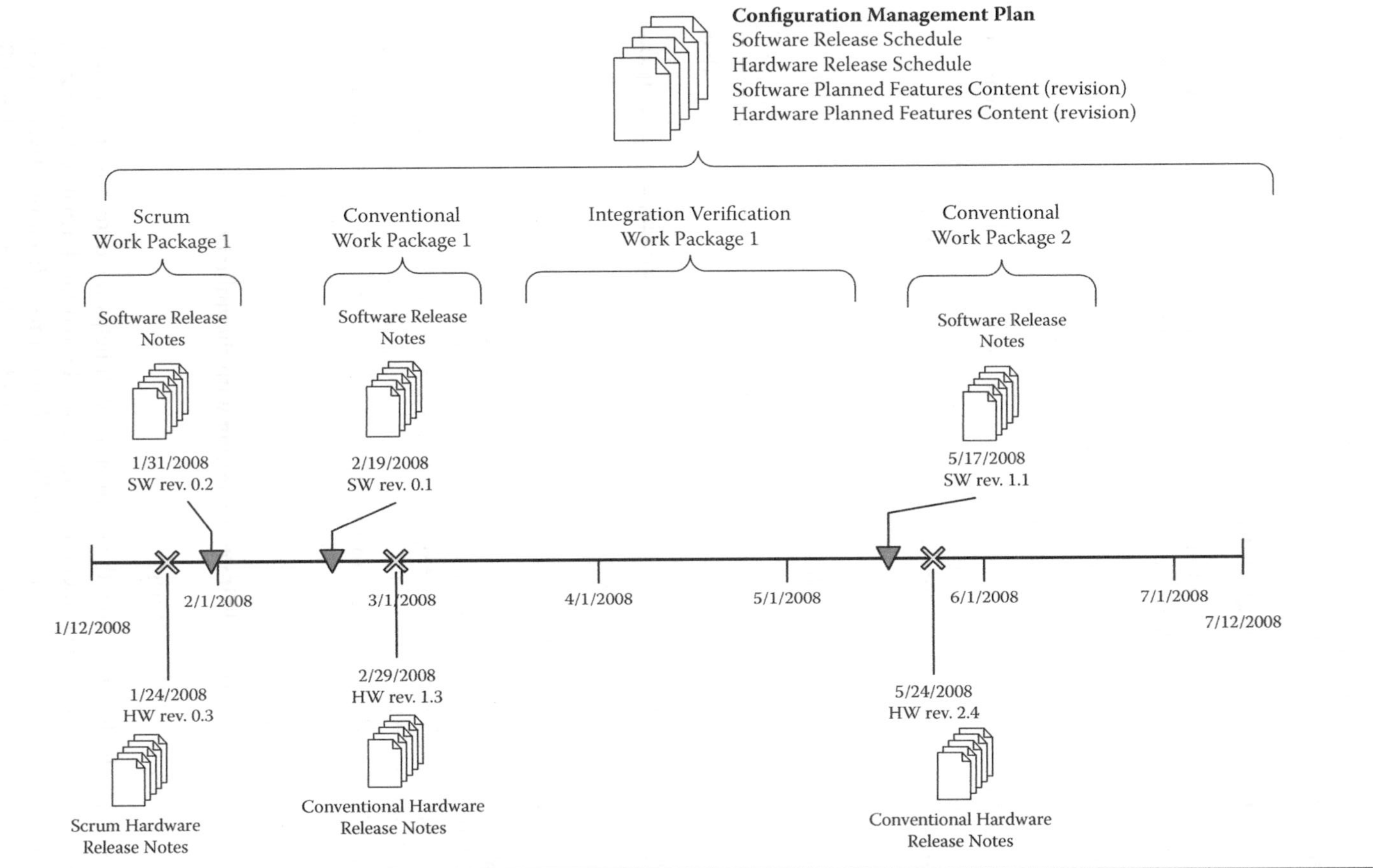

Figure 9.2 Configuration management.

the scrum teams. The functional configuration audit is a means by which the government agency or department can verify that the product or process functions as required in the product specification.

9.3.4.5 Interface Management

Interface management becomes important when the government function uses a collection of contractors to deliver the final product. If the interfaces are not well-defined from the start of the project, it is unlikely the completed system will function as expected. If the program is extremely large, the systems engineering function for the program managers will have to manage interfaces composed of various contractors. That is interface management at the human level as opposed to the physical design of the product. Once the human resources are under control, we also need to manage the interfaces in the software and interfaces in the hardware, particularly if we are dealing with a significant number of subsystems (think "aircraft carrier").

9.3.4.6 Data Management

If substantial data management hardware will be needed for the program, we will not use the scrum approach for that part of the activity. Scrum teams will generally protect their intellectual property by using some kind of formal configuration management system. In large government contracts, we may find a regulatory requirement that forces us to use substantial hardware resources in order to manage data. If we are dealing with the military, they may have pre-existing data requirements that will not change because we are using a scrum team for development.

9.3.4.7 Systems Engineering Master Schedule (SEMS)

The systems engineering master schedule is sometimes called the Integrated Master Plan. This planning document sits atop all other schedules and coordinates the program. Individual contractors develop their own schedules, which will be subordinate to the Integrated Master Plan. The goal of the Integrated Master Plan is to ensure that all phases and contributors to the project are synchronized. The existence of this plan does not agitate against the use of the scrum approach. If the plan is naive, it may lead to a simplistic waterfall method and we have already discussed the defects of this approach. Once again, we may be constrained by the requirements of the government agency, especially if we are dealing with the military.

9.3.4.8 Response to Change

We have already discussed how the scrum approach helps the enterprise to manage change. Although the government agencies generally require formal configuration management in order to protect the intellectual investment from the development work as well as to ensure delivery of the proper product, the scrum approach will fit into this formality as well as any other technique.

As usual, the short planning horizon and the rapid tempo will allow the scrum teams to flex with requirements changes. The use of configuration management or product data management software reduces the pain for all parties and provides an audit trail for the documentation.

9.4 Systems Engineering Output

9.4.1 Specifications and Baselines

Specifications and baselines will generally be developed by the systems engineering function. That is not to say that the scrum teams cannot perform this function, but most government contracts will expect significant systems engineering involvement during this particular phase of the project. In the case where baselines are set up to be milestones, the scrum teams will have no involvement at all. Note that we often will find in the literature that the words *specification* and *requirements* will be used indiscriminately and as synonyms. A specification is a documentary instantiation of a requirement for a set of related requirements.

9.4.2 Life Cycle Support Data

Government projects will require significant measurement requirements in the form of metrics. At a minimum, the project manager will be reporting the results of earned value management. The contract may potentially demand even more metrics than those provided by the project manager. For example, the software developers, whether they are scrum teams or not, have to supply data that describes their productivity as well as their failure rates (sometimes called defect density). Printed circuit board developers may have to provide data regarding the number of board turns as well as the electromagnetic compatibility results derived from design verification testing.

While we often think of the scrum approach as a tool for developing a product, we can also use the method to support the product through the life cycle from launch to product retirement. If the product has a long life span (some commercial vehicle companies expect twenty years of support!), we can anticipate changes in the membership of the scrum team with the attendant training to bring new members up to speed with the rest of the team.

9.5 Systems Engineering Planning

9.5.1 Systems Engineering Management Plan (SEMP)

The systems engineering management plan is an umbrella name for a collection of tools designed to drive the project to timely success. While the activity of scrum teams may fall under the various schedules and plans, the development of the schedules and plans is not an activity in the scrum approach.

9.5.2 Technical Performance Measurement (TPM) Planning

Technical performance measurement is one of the items that differentiates systems engineering from standard project management. We can use the product backlog, sprint backlogs, and the burndown charts as evidence of progress in technical development of the product.

9.5.3 Systems Engineering Detailed Schedule (SEDS)

The SEDS fits well with the scrum approach to the extent that we are dealing with a work breakdown structure decomposed to the "atomic" level. If the detailed plan is a long-range plan, which is likely on large products, we can expect the actual consumption of the product backlog to lag behind the plan as reality meets expectation. As long as all the players understand that this separation between expected results and real delivery is likely to occur, we are unlikely to see a punitive response toward the development teams.

The developers of the SEDS must understand the concept of the sellable product because the iterations will become part of the detailed schedule. The sellable product concept easily tops the schedule itself as a tool for reducing risk.

9.6 Functional Tasks

9.6.1 Reliability and Maintainability

Reliability and maintainability testing can consume an immense amount of resources—human, material, and financial. We see no reason why the scrum approach cannot be used during reliability and maintainability testing, including planning as well as execution. In fact, one of the authors uses the scrum approach precisely for this purpose. One of the difficulties with reliability and maintainability testing lies with the long durations required in order to deliver information about the expected life of the product. In many cases, these tests can go on for months. That means the scrum meetings and the sprint reviews are more likely to be status reports than planning for execution—especially once the testing has commenced.

Hence, reliability and maintainability testing has a significant amount of risk. This risk is difficult to mitigate and the scrum approach will not provide as much assistance in this case as it would in other portions of the development process. Why is that? The reason lies in the fact that we are only reporting status of a test or a bank of tests rather than continuously executing. In other words, once these tests commence, the scrum teams will have little to do but watch the progress of the various tests.

9.6.2 Survivability

Survivability is perhaps a more complex topic than reliability and maintainability. It is easy to see how it relates to military projects but it may be a little bit more difficult to generalize than the concept of reliability and maintainability. On the other hand, we have recommended for years that all suppliers and customers perform tests to destruction rather than stopping at the design limit and reporting results as a binary attribute—pass or fail. The moment our test teams mature to destructive testing, they are analyzing the product for survivability.

As with reliability and maintainability testing, scrum teams can be used to monitor and develop these tests also. If the test environment is especially severe, the tests will be of short duration and the scrum teams will be more involved in the execution rather than simply reporting the progress of the tests. Testing to destruction is the only way to ensure that the scrum test teams have covered testing to the design limit, testing to failure, and testing to destruction. Without test to destruction, what do we really know about the product? It doesn't really matter whether the product is a weapons system, a commercial vehicle, or a new software application. The goal of this kind of testing is to find out when and where it fails. Obviously, we don't want any product, government or otherwise, to fail at a point that is close to the design limit; that is to say, in order to have a margin of safety, we expected a destruct point to be significantly beyond the design limit.

9.6.3 Electromagnetic Compatibility and Radio Frequency Management

We currently use the scrum concept in a commercial vehicle supplier laboratory to perform electromagnetic compatibility and radio frequency testing. One of the noticeable improvements—within a couple of weeks—was the acceleration of the pace of test completion. The expected improvement in tempo occurred quickly as the members of the team began to answer the three questions in the daily meeting and drive down the sprint backlog. For a laboratory environment, we are looking at line management; hence, the product backlog is a rolling backlog because we are adding new activities frequently. Project-style product backlogs generally have a beginning, a middle, and an end.

9.6.4 Human Factors

Human factors analysis is one of those checklist items in a government standard that ensures that some level of attention be paid to human-machine interactions and not be forgotten. Since human factors analysis requires testing and we already know that testing fits into the scrum approach, we can assume it will work just as well for human factors analysis as it does for any other form of testing. Since human factors testing and analysis is a specialty, the team must have some members that have that specific expertise. Other than that, the scrum approach, including the sprints in the daily scrum meetings, should proceed as we have described throughout this book.

9.6.5 System Safety and Health Hazard

System safety and health hazard analysis is another test function. The scrum approach should work here as well and once again we need to ensure that our teams have the correct expertise so that we get the results we expect. Some government agencies may expect the hazard analysis and critical control point approach used by the food and drug industries. This approach uses control plans and failure mode and effects analyses very much like the automotive industry does in the United States. In addition, several military standards explicitly describe the approach that should be used for military projects.

9.6.6 System Security

What is system security? With information technology, we are talking about information security. With commercial vehicles for the military, we must implement security features. This can involve providing secure vehicles, instrument panel blackout ability, and hardened wire harnesses. In addition, we want to maintain the security of the project itself so the whole concept of system security is multimodal and, thanks to the responsibility involved, may not be a good choice for the scrum approach unless the entire scrum team has the appropriate clearances. Frequently, security functions for military and other sensitive projects will be centralized with one group. Keeping the function to one group can help prevent the leaks that might occur when we have miscommunication among a variety of teams.

9.6.7 Producibility

Producibility is not often a responsibility for the scrum teams. As always, the scrum approach could be used to maintain the intensity of the activity. We must pay attention to regulatory requirements and not blindly proceed with the scrum approach if, for whatever reason, it is inappropriate. Producibility is often called design for manufacture and assembly (DFMA). If we can break this task down into small enough tasks, we can use scrum teams to go through the analyses by formulating the tasks into product and sprint backlogs. The only caveat is that the members of the team have the appropriate qualifications to perform the task.

9.6.8 Integrated Logistics Support (ILS)

Integrated logistics support is typical of military projects. The government wants to be sure that deliveries occur promptly and as expected. As with any function, we could use scrum teams to perform the actual task. Most commonly, however, this task will be planned by the systems engineer in concert with the procurement function, which usually includes shipping. Hence, the system engineer is responsible for creating the product backlog and may also have a hand in the spring backlogs.

9.6.9 Test and Evaluation

The overall test and evaluation planning for a large program is typically a responsibility of the systems engineering function. However, the detailed activities that fall under the overall heading of test and evaluation can be managed well using the scrum approach.

During a major development project between a commercial vehicle manufacturer and an electronic supplier, both authors use the concept of a Test and Evaluation Master Plan (TEMP) to devise an approach for the development of product software that was effectively a primitive version of the scrum approach. We define a collection of software packages each of which was a superset of the previous release (see Figure 9.3). The first software package would have core software that would support all subsequent packages. The idea was that the core should have the hooks to attach the software of the next layer. Our expectation was that any failures would principally occur in the most recent layer. By proposing a multitude of concentric software packages, we were reducing risk while always having releasable software ready to go. This approach is very similar to the mentality used when applying scrum. While not all of us are releasing weapon systems, the concept of the TEMP generalizes easily.

The scrum teams will most likely develop their architecture of software packages in the first few sprints. They may also develop their plan for verification and validation. Note that the tests in the validation master plan are a reasonable approach, meet government requirements, and allow the freedom to implement a scrum verification and validation model.

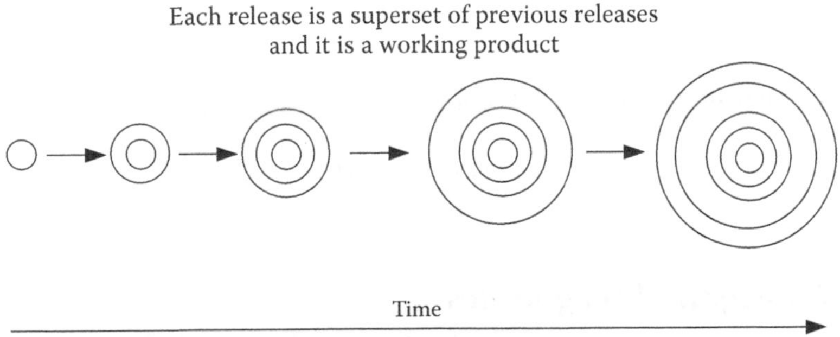
Each release is a superset of previous releases
and it is a working product
Time

Figure 9.3 Onion-model for product, process, or service releases.

1. System introduction
   a. Mission description
   b. System threat assessment
   c. Minimum acceptable operational performance requirements
   d. System description
   e. Critical technical parameters
2. Integrated test program summary
   a. Integrated test program schedule
   b. Management
3. Developmental test and evaluation outline (please note that we perform developmental testing in order to provide ourselves with some confidence in the design)
   a. Developmental test and evaluation overview
   b. Developmental test and evaluation to date
   c. Future developmental test and evaluation
   d. Live fire test and evaluation (equivalent to severe field testing with civilian products)
4. Operational test and evaluation outline (note here that we perform operational testing in order to validate the product—testing our manufacturing process and all the support systems that go into producing the product)
   a. Operational test and evaluation overview
   b. Critical operational issues
   c. Operational test and evaluation to date
   d. Future operational test and evaluation
5. Test and evaluation resource summary
   a. Test articles—best articles are often called unit under test or UUT
   b. Test sites and instrumentation
   c. Test support equipment—test support equipment usually refers to the fixtures that we will need in order to execute the test; we may not need fixtures in the case where we have a full system test in a live scenario
   d. Threat systems/simulators
   e. Test targets and expendable items—with military projects, test targets can become expensive, particularly when the target is a main battle tank or a jet fighter plane
   f. Operational force test support
   g. Simulations, models, and test beds
   h. Special requirements
   i. Test and evaluation funding requirements
   j. Manpower/personnel training

9.6.10 Integrated Diagnostics

Anytime we see the term "integrated" in a government standard, especially military standards, we can anticipate that this is a systems engineering activity. Integrated diagnostics represent another function that must be managed among a multiplicity of contractors and a variety of interfaces. For every system and subsystem to "talk" with each other, higher-level management must be engaged to avoid the inevitable babel that occurs when communications management is overlooked. We would not expect this particular function, at least in the planning stages, to be a scrum activity. During the execution phase, we see no reason why scrum cannot be used as long as executive management provides a level of oversight—perhaps with a scrum of scrums.

9.6.11 Transportability

Transportability is particularly significant when dealing with very large weapons systems; for example, a main battle tank. Transportability should be defined during the planning phases of the project and can be a reasonable choice for the scrum approach, particularly if we are talking about eighty-ton requirements.

The requirements can decompose into a product backlog in the following way:

- Product package
  - Dimensions
  - Weight
  - Peculiar characteristics
  - Hazardous substance requirements
- Product packaging
  - Container size
  - Pallet use
  - Less-than-loaded (LTL) considerations
- Transporting spares
  - Spare containers
  - Spare size
  - Spare weight
- Shipping type
  - Air transport
  - Ships
  - Rail
  - Commercial vehicle
    - Class
    - Trailer
    - One-piece
    - Allowed routes

9.6.12 Infrastructure Support

Infrastructure support is another program item that can represent a vast amount of resources. For example, when we deal with the weapon system, logistics, spares, training, and other ongoing activities will require some kind of infrastructure to support that weapon system. One example of such a system is the patriot anti-aircraft artillery system. These systems are extremely complex and they have a substantial infrastructure to support their development and maintenance.

Software products also require support for some kind of maintenance infrastructure. We have never seen product software that didn't require either updating or upgrading or both. This idea supports the existence of a sustaining engineering group. Such a group is part of the support infrastructure that we have already discussed. Sustaining engineering activities fit into the scrum approach easily. We ran a sustaining team using the scrum approach: the sustaining activities functioned as a rolling product backlog, which we decomposed into sprint backlogs.

9.6.13 Other Functional Areas

Any other functional areas that are part of the program will require both planning and execution and possibly follow-through. In all cases, we may be able to gracefully use the scrum approach to manage the execution phase of the development for each functional area.

9.7 Leveraged Options

The government uses the term "leveraged options" to refer to the situations when existing products or software can be used to support the mission of the program. Leverage options are a form of sustaining engineering as well as a risk-reducing choice.

9.7.1 Non-Developmental Items (NDIs)

A non-developmental item is a product that already exists. We can expect to occasionally see the term "commercial off-the-shelf" or COTS. Clearly, if a product already exists, then a substantial amount of development time can be eliminated by the beginning of the project. The selection of NDIs will most likely be the responsibility of the systems engineering function; however, we can use scrum teams during the execution phase by treating these NDIs as if they were sustaining engineering projects.

9.7.2 Open System Architectures (OSAs)

Open system architectures can perhaps best be exemplified by an operating system such as Linux. One of the benefits of these architectures is that they are well-defined and well-documented; one of the defects of these architectures is that they are publicly well-documented. If the information is readily available to the public and we are developing a military product, then we may have security issues. As usual, the execution phase of this activity can easily implement the scrum approach.

9.7.3 Reuse

Reuse is one of the holy grails of software development. Existing and well-tested code represents a speedy and safe way to bypass a large amount of risky and potentially slow software development. Reuse can be implemented in the form of libraries or object-oriented code or both. Software development, including the use of libraries, is almost always an activity for which the scrum approach applies. Since scrum came from agile software development, it makes sense that we apply it to software reuse as well.

9.8 Pervasive Development Considerations

9.8.1 Computer Resources

We see no reason not to use scrum teams for the development of computer resources to support the program. We expect the rate of reporting to reduce the risk. As we know already, the scrum approach arose from agile software development practices, so the use in this venue is natural for dealing with computer resources.

9.8.2 Materials, Processes, and Parts Control

Materials, processes, and parts control are all part of traditional manufacturing considerations. Again, we can use the scrum team approach with these traditional activities. However, we may have to define a policy for materials, processes, and parts control at the systems level. We would do this to ensure consistency across the program. Once we have consistent policies and procedures, we can activate scrum teams and derive the benefit of high-intensity execution.

9.8.3 Prototyping

Prototyping is an activity we perform to produce prereleased versions of the final product for a variety of purposes:

- Providing sample products for design verification
- Using the prototypes for manufacturing development
- Checking out form, fit, and partial function with the customer: military or civilian
- Working with suppliers and subcontractors

An architect, Paul Discoe,[1] said "In order to find out what you don't know, it is useful to do something once," referring to prototyping. Since prototyping is a subset of the development activities, we can use a scrum team with the appropriate skill sets to design, develop, and test the prototypes at any phase in the project.

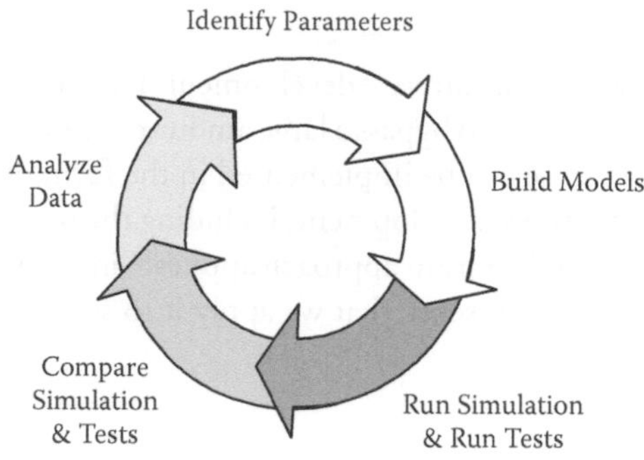

Figure 9.4 Simulation.

9.8.4 Simulation

Simulation can be a software development process in its own right. Hardware simulators are also a separate development process and any hybridization between software and hardware to produce a simulator is likely to be a major development process. Because the scrum approach is strongly oriented toward development of new products, the approach will fit well with any kind of simulator development. We strongly recommend the use of simulators whenever possible. A well-developed simulator provides the ability to test long before final software or final hardware is available for the test bench for field testing. Furthermore, simulation allows us to execute what-if scenarios without destroying our product, our fixtures, or our test environment. Really good simulators allow us to do strange things such as send illegal messages over data buses that normally do not allow that kind of behavior or we may even be able to set up "impossible" hardware scenarios (see Figure 9.4).

One of the caveats of developing for simulators, using scrum or conventional teams, is that the members of the simulator development team should not be members of the development team for the full product. Our experience suggests that having common individuals on both teams can lead to an "incestuous" development situation where both the product and the simulator work together well, but the product will not work properly in the field. Hence, the definition of interfaces among the various subsystems is particularly critical if we want to develop a good functional simulator. The human interfaces need to be controlled on the scrum teams to avoid this negative cross-fertilization.

9.9 System/Cost Effectiveness

9.9.1 Manufacturing Analysis and Assessment

Manufacturing analysis and assessment is not a military-only activity although it is certainly part of the release of any kind of system. In the automotive world, this analysis and assessment, as well as the execution of manufacturing development and design, are explicitly part of the advanced product quality planning process.

9.9.2 Verification Analysis and Assessment

The manpower to execute verification analysis and assessment should use a TEMP (also known as the product backlog for verification). We see no reason why the scrum approach can't be used to deal with verification analysis and assessment. As with any case where we use scrum in a military or government project, we will have to synchronize the actions of the scrum teams with any other teams that may be working on the project, and, as with the waterfall approach, it would probably be best if we held meetings to synchronize all the teams. Verification analysis and assessment occurs when we take the results of our design and operational test, and subject them to more sophisticated analyses than simply reporting results.

9.9.3 Deployment Analysis and Assessment

When we perform deployment analysis and assessment, we are taking a look at how the final product could be distributed to the end customers. With military projects, the deployment may be global. The same thing is certainly true of very large trans-national corporations and even some medium-size corporations in the global marketplace. We should also consider the need for spares, updates, and upgrades in our plans for deployment of the product. Again, scrum teams can certainly perform the execution phase of this task, particularly since we are talking about analysis and assessment and not a large-scale consumption of resources.

9.9.4 Operational Analysis and Assessment

Operational analysis and assessment will occur naturally if we are looking at the behavior of the product: the quality and the reliability. The same thing will occur with civilian companies and nonmilitary government agencies. We already use scrum teams to perform reliability analyses and we anticipate no significant issues when the same approach is applied to challenges with quality. Usually, operational analysis and assessment will lead to some modicum of corrective action, and, if we are truly proactive, will move toward preventive actions as well.

Whether the customer is a government agency or not is not really germane to this kind of analysis and assessment. What is germane is a rapid and complete response on the supplier or contractor side. It is bad enough that the customer already has an issue with the product. If the contractor is truly proactive, they will already have a failure reporting and corrective action system in place with suitable verification and validation built into the process. The failure reporting and corrective action system can be maintained by a scrum with a rolling product backlog.

9.9.5 Supportability Analysis and Assessment

The concept of supportability implies we have a product that will be available for a substantial time. In the commercial vehicle business, we often expect to support vehicles for at least twenty years with contractually defined service parts. If the commercial vehicles will be used in developing nations, we can expect the vehicle to last another ten years. Such is also the case with military programs; for example, the B-52 strategic bomber first rolled off the assembly line in 1954. That means we may have had some of the aircraft in the air in one form or another for fifty-five years! When we use parts for half a century, the idea of supportability analysis and assessment seems more important. We see no reason why the scrum approach cannot be used for this particular activity much as we have described its use with sustaining engineering. We expect the usual improvements or reporting, accelerated tempo, and prompt execution.

9.9.6 Training Analysis and Assessment

Training is an often-overlooked part of large programs. Not only do we need to analyze and assess what training must occur, but we must also analyze and assess the benefits we presumably received post-training. If we assume we are using subject matter experts as members of the team, a scrum team approach will work for training analysis and assessment.

9.9.7 Disposal Analysis and Assessment

With military products, we may have some problems related to the final disposition of the product. For example, if we are dealing with munitions, we have a responsibility to dispose of the product safely. With informational products such as computers and computer software, we can have security issues while trying to dispose of the product. In general, specific rules apply to products that have security issues. Appropriate disposition will most likely require a team of subject matter experts. Once we have those experts, they can become members of the scrum team to execute the disposition of these dangerous products.

We don't often see disposal analysis and assessment in civilian product development. It would be simple to task a scrum team with this action at the beginning of a project. Since we deal with vehicle electronics, many of which still contained lead-based solder joints, safe disposal has become a regulatory issue. Most electronic firms in North America are engaged in a shift from leaded to unleaded solder formulations.

9.9.8 Environmental Analysis and Impact Assessment

In some ways, environmental analysis and impact assessments are a superset of disposal analysis and assessment, particularly in the age of "green" initiatives. We will need subject matter experts on our scrum teams in order to execute these analyses and assessments. Once subject matter experts have been secured, we can temporarily form a scrum team to execute the analyses and assessments. They can disband at the completion of the task and reform as needed on other projects.

9.9.9 Life Cycle Cost Analysis and Assessment

Life cycle cost analysis and assessment will most likely be performed by the financial function of the organization—in many cases, the accounting department or the finance directorate. In some cases, life cycle costing is primarily a reporting activity. However, the finance team will also have some responsibility for projecting future costs, particularly for long-lived products.

9.10 Military Reviews

The U.S. Department of Defense specifies (MIL-STD-1521B) a sequence of technical reviews for projects that involve either software or hardware (see Figure 9.5). The following list shows the general sequence:

- System requirements reviews
- System design review
- Software specification review
- Preliminary design review
- Critical design review
- Test readiness reviews
- Functional configuration audit
- Physical configuration audit
- Formal qualification review
- Production readiness review

If we are going to use the scrum approach, we will have to accommodate a formal review sequence as specified above. As of this writing, the standard for these reviews has been available for thirty-three years. Even when these standards are retired by the Department of Defense, practitioners still follow the general sequence. In order to implement scrum with this kind of sequence, we will need to synchronize the sprints with the formal reviews.

Figure 9.6 shows a very simple version of a government program. This figure shows how scrum fits in with a more complex military program.

We think it is clear that the scrum approach can be used with Defense project management as easily as it can be used with any other kind of project management technique.

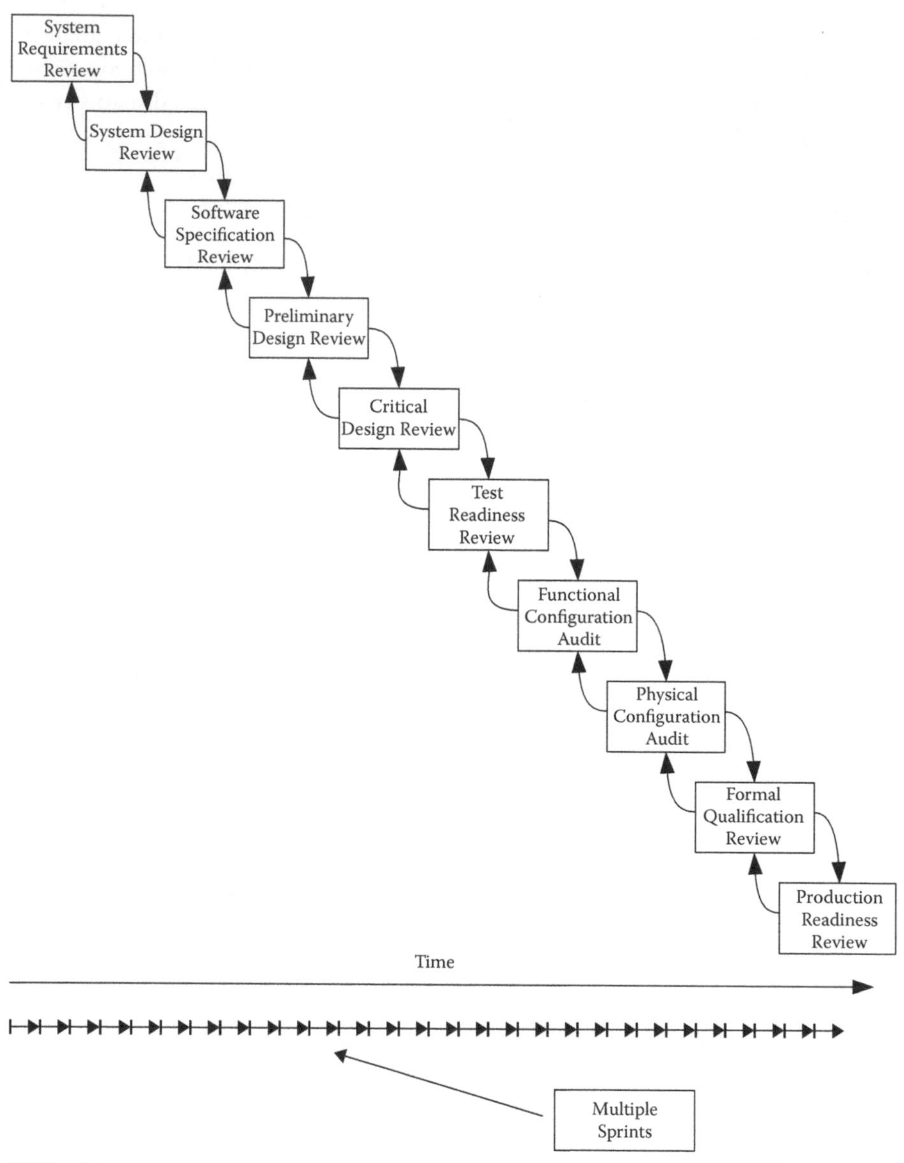

Figure 9.5 MIL-STD-1521B program with sprints.

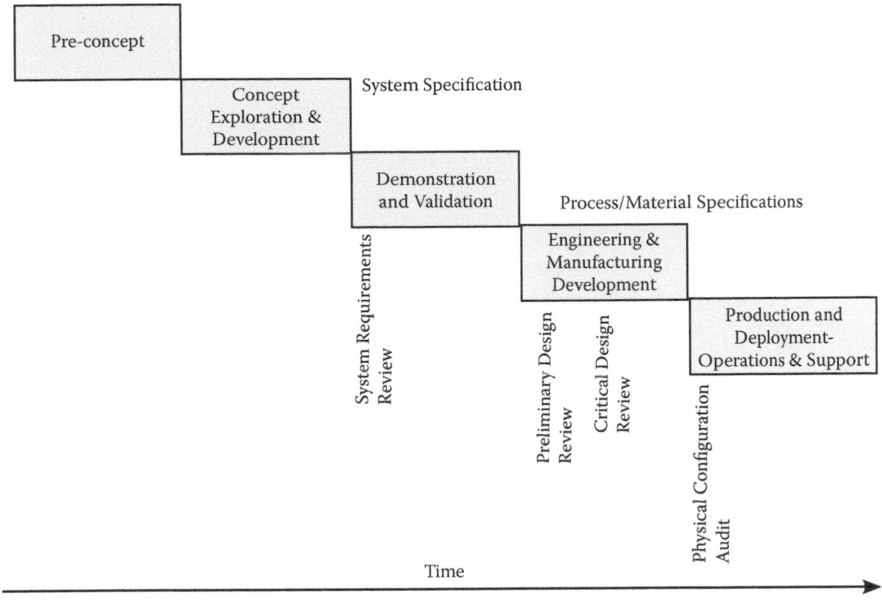

Figure 9.6 Abstract representation of a military program.

Note

1. Paul Discoe, *Zen Architecture: the Building Process as Practice*, (Layton, UT: Gibbs Smith 2008), 206

Chapter 10

Scrum and Service Industry

We would like to avoid giving the impression that the scrum approach can only be used in manufacturing. Our educational example is one version of what we can do with the scrum approach while providing a specific kind of service. We feel that the higher intensity and tempo acceleration provide significant advantages for any team in the service industries.

10.1 The Service Industry

The primary sector of any economy provides raw materials for the secondary sector, which is generally considered to be manufacturing. The so-called tertiary sector of economy provides services to businesses as well as final consumers. These services may involve the transport, distribution, and sale of goods from producer to an end consumer as we see with wholesaling and retailing, or may involve the sale of something we would generally understand to be a service, such as with child-care or janitorial services (see Figure 10.1). Some people think of an electrical utility as a service, but that industry breaks out into (1) generation, which includes the manufacture of power and (2) transmission and distribution, which transports and distributes the power to customers (a service). Most of the time, then, we are looking at a product that is an action rather than something we can see or hold in our hands.

We should also note that when the revenue of services exceeds that of the raw material and manufacturing sectors, we will sometimes say we are in a "post-industrial society." Typically, postindustrial societies reside in North America, northern Europe, and some of the Asian countries. As a note of interest, some services requiring substantial cognitive skills are called the quaternary sector.

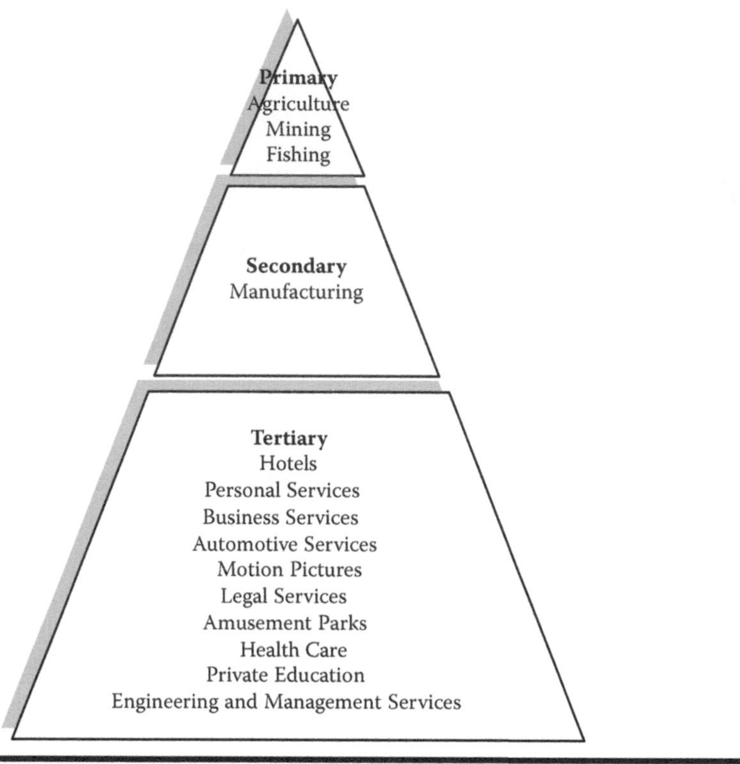

Figure 10.1 Service industry.

The so-called quinary sector might be construed to be government services. We feel that the last two sector definitions are redundant.

10.2 Products of the Service Industry

As we indicated, the product of the service industry is usually the service itself. This situation makes the service industry a transaction-based industry; that is, much of the action occurs person-to-person. In the service industry, it generally does not make much sense to base costing on direct labor although this is still a large part of cost accounting. For example, the product of a consultant may be the use of knowledge skills, where we have no real raw material and no manufacturing.

Software development is another ambiguous area because the product is a knowledge product for the most part and a true manufactured product in the traditional sense when embedded or sold as a package. Although software may be packaged in a manufacturing facility, the software itself is a collection of code. We think the scrum approach can be used for any small to medium project for any industry.

Often, the service industry will be broken in "sectors," comprised of:

- Finance
- Insurance
- Real estate
- Retail
- Transportation
- Public utilities
- Wholesale
- Distribution (may be pushed into wholesale)
- Education
- Health
- Information technology
- Food service
- Miscellaneous services

10.3 Defining Processes in the Service Industry

One approach to defining processes in the service industries would be to use a quality function deployment (QFD) to establish the voice of the customer. The voice of the customer is important when selling a manufactured product. When selling a service, it is even more important due to the "soft" nature of the service. These transactional activities are amenable to the use of scrum teams, who can participate in the following activities:

- Quality function deployment
- Pugh concept selection
- Opinion surveys
  - Mail-out
  - In-person
  - Telephone
  - Internet
- Ethnographic methods

A top-level product backlog for a scrum team for capturing the voice of the customer can look like the following:

1. Set goals and objectives
2. Set schedule and budget
3. Preliminary work with a focus group
4. Set population and sampling rules
5. Assess expectations regarding missing data
6. Procedures for population and sampling
7. Design survey

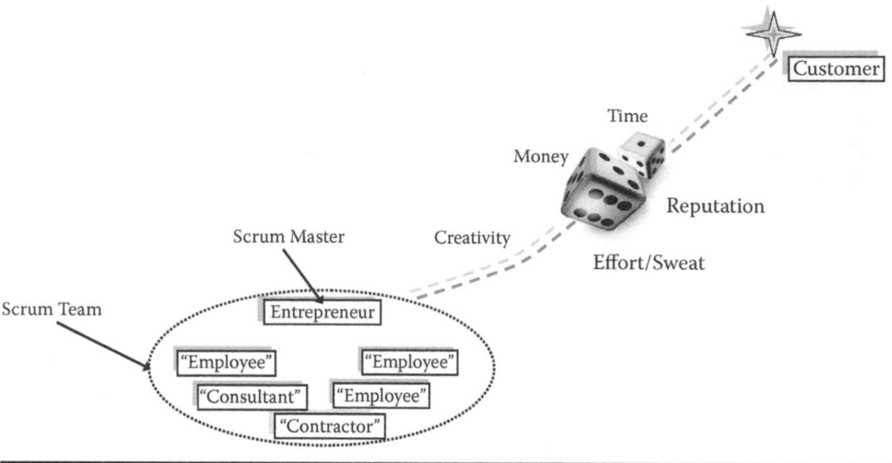

Figure 10.2 Scrum applied to the service industry.

8. Pretest survey
9. Select interviewers
10. Execute the survey
11. Analyze the survey

10.4 Deploying Scrum in the Service Industry

Now we know what the service industry is and how it fits into the economy. Because the scrum team approach is a project-oriented approach, any venue that uses projects to accomplish goals is a candidate for use of the scrum approach (see Figure 10.2). The only real difference is that the product in this venue is a task rather than an object.

Consider an organization that wants to launch a new service for their customers. Maybe a customer has approached the organization with a proposal that starts like "it sure would be nice if you guys would. . . ." The service may have a number of technical aspects and user stories that will need to be considered. The organization can identify and set priorities for the introduction of the user stories into the organization with those customers and the appropriate scrum team. We then lay out the user stories and tasks in priority and dependency order to create the product backlog and then proceed to develop the sprint backlogs, daily meetings, and burndown charts.

10.5 Benefits of Scrum in the Service Industry

One of the benefits discussed earlier is the money brought into the organization even as the development work is ongoing. Correctly setting priorities for the user stories in relation to customer needs and quick delivery allows for the possibility of generating cash flow early in the process, paying off any expenditure to develop the feature or service. Additionally, the close interaction with the customer helps ensure that what is delivered is what the customer needs.

Regardless of business type, we use the scrum approach to define a set of deliverables in which we have a sellable product at every release, whether that product is a service, hardware, software, or a mixture. Clearly, the early releases will have minimal functionality—but they *will* be functional! Early delivery also means early testing; early testing means early elimination of observed defects. Early delivery means we beat the market on delivery while generating cash flow much earlier than a conventional project.

Obviously, when the scrum approach is tied in with a waterfall or systems engineering model, we may not be able to accept purchase orders until much later in the project. Even so, we will be able to test much earlier with a working version than we otherwise would do.

10.6 Examples of Scrum in the Service Industry

Suppose we are restaurateurs and we want to offer a new product to our customers. Possibly our customers have even requested a new dinner or product. We ask our customers more about the quality and attributes of this dish they "wish we had."

After we begin to understand the customer expectation, we want to purchase any new equipment it would take to deliver the product. We want to spend some time with this new equipment to understand how it works and gain some confidence with working with the tool. We may research different recipes for how to make the product. Finally, we would plan to deliver the first pass of the product without any customization or add-ons. When we believe we have the first pass of the product, we may offer it to some of our key customers for their feedback on the entree. Their feedback and that of our restaurant team can have some constructive additions (ingredients or side items) or possible product permutations. These adaptations may be integrated into the product and then we can offer this new variation. We repeat our testing and modifications until the product is clearly successful and our customers are showing evidence of enjoying it enough to be willing to pay for it.

The point here is the scrum approach need not be limited to software or highly technical projects. The methods can be applied to any sort of project. We have shown how we can adapt the scrum approach for nearly any industry. The reason we can do this adaptation is because the scrum approach *always* fits within the review sequence of any major project methodology or industry. The scope and sequence will remain unchanged while we reap the benefits of improved tempo.

Chapter 11

Scrum and Hospitals

Hospitals are similar to the educational system in that they have multiple chains of command, some of which are roughly equivalent.

11.1 Levels

The various chains of command in a modern hospital can sometimes make cross-functional teamwork a trying experience. Figure 11.1 is an extremely simplified version of an organizational chart.

We don't advocate cross-functional teams just to have cross-functional teams; however, the use of team members from other functions may lead to improved communications among the various functions as well as the potential for serendipitous innovations related to the dialectical relation among the players. Because the daily scrum meetings are very short, they shouldn't interfere with routine hospital work.

11.1.1 Hospital Management

Hospital management will have its own agenda, usually related to profit as well as to operational considerations. The use of scrum teams with this group would be very much as it is with any other group about which we have written. Since the purpose of the hospital includes the concept of medicine, it only makes sense to create cross-functional teams that include not only the operational individuals, but the nurse and physicians also. Obviously, we want to use good judgment with regard to the amount of time the direct medical practitioners spend away from their patients.

Hospital management departments can build cross-functional teams from the operational departments quickly. Cross-pollination will allow for at least an understanding of each other's responsibilities. Administrative initiatives should follow the usual scrum pattern and begin to close out more frequently as the rate of project accomplishment increases.

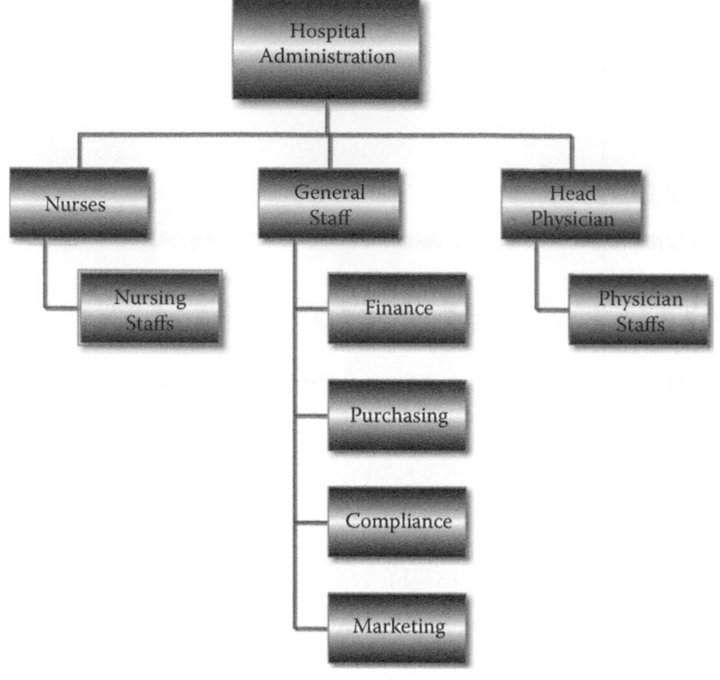

Figure 11.1 Hospital staffing.

11.1.2 Physicians

The use of the scrum approach with physicians may meet resistance since it does not follow any of the traditional management paradigms with which the doctors are acquainted. Nonetheless, the approach can be explained in a short training course and pilot teams used before deploying the concept hospital-wide.

We know, for example, recent work has been done related to washing hands in hospitals. Physicians and nurses often get tired of all the handwashing because it begins to cause skin damage around the cuticles in addition to occasionally severe chapping. The soaps used in hospitals tend to be powerful antibacterials, so the depredations to the skin are not trivial. On the other hand, the failure to wash hands can lead to potentially fatal infections, just as it did as late as the nineteenth century when the idea of washing hands was considered to be radical. The scrum approach would provide a high-speed, minimally invasive way for physicians to get involved in a handwashing initative.

Doctors, like nurses, have responsibility for clients/patients. The scrum approach should in no way affect this responsibility negatively. Our experience suggests the opposite is more likely. Because internal initiatives will be completed sooner, the doctors should have more time and less stress when dealing with patients.

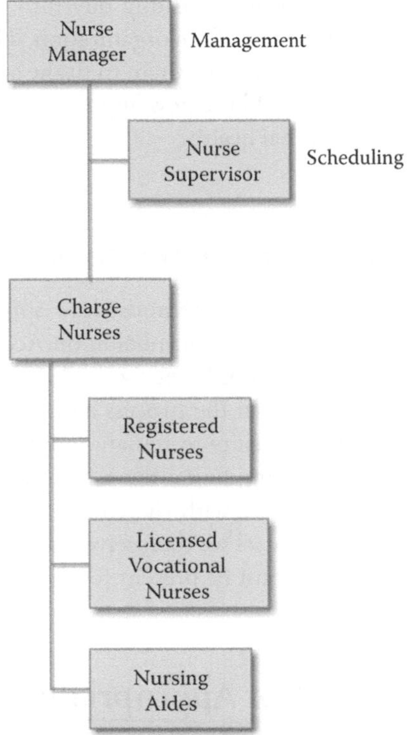

Figure 11.2 Nurse staffing.

11.1.3 Nurses

Figure 11.2 shows one model for nurse staffing. The nurse manager (once called a "head nurse") provides direction and management for a given unit. The nurse supervisor, in this model, is responsible for scheduling the shift work for the various levels of nurses and aides. Sometimes the nurse supervisors spend the bulk of their time inveigling staff members to come in and work overtime, which can produce quality issues. Registered nurses are more highly trained than the licensed vocational (or "practical") nurses and are usually able to dispense medications, a legal requirement for the license. Nursing aides provide support and may help to move patients.

Given the scheduling issues and other health-related projects, the scrum approach can work well with the nursing units. One difficulty may be including people from the various shifts (hospitals often run day, swing, and night shifts; others have sixteen-hour shifts). The team may have to use virtual scrum to communicate, although they may decide that the sprint period meetings (retrospective and planning) should have all hands in attendance.

All teams, including the nursing team, should measure the completion rate of projects. If they can prove to themselves that the scrum approach improves the rate of attainment of projects, they will more readily buy into the methodology and, perhaps, become evangelists for the rest of the organization. The trickiest part of this process with nurses will be finding a way for them to fit the activities into their busy workday schedules. At no point should the new approach be putting someone's life at risk or driving them to suboptimal health.

11.2 Types of Projects Amenable to Scrum

Projects can be chosen from Six Sigma methods, lean approaches, or regulatory requirements needs (for example, Joint Commission on Accreditation of Hospital Organizations [JCAHO] compliance). Obviously, both Six Sigma and lean manufacturing provide for improvement in the process and product, whereas meeting regulatory requirements allows the facility to remain in business. Since team meetings are already common with nursing units, the scrum teams will not come as a shock. The biggest problems may arise with the culture clash between nurses and physicians, particularly given that nurses see themselves as the primary care providers based on the amount of time they must be present for the patients.

11.3 Where Scrum Is Not Appropriate

We suspect it is unlikely for the scrum approach to be popular in the operating rooms and emergency areas, although we see no fundamental reason why the approach would not provide the same benefits as it does in every other area. In many ways, the scrum approach is like any other project management technique, but with a higher cadence and reduced risk due to the information flowing through the teams.

We believe the decision should be made when considering the perception of the clients/patients who may look on scrum as a dangerous experiment and miss the point of the reduced risk. Covert scrum usage could backfire; however, since many quality projects are not publicized in hospitals, ignorance of the use of scrum might be considered to be a sin of omission.

Chapter 12

Outsourced Scrum

12.1 Distributed Teams

We can visualize at least four possible models for global teaming:

- On-site, where we move the team to a customer location
- Onshore, where we move the team to a home country, often the United States
- Nearshore, where we move the team to a nearby country—for the United States this would usually be Mexico or Canada
- Offshore, where the work is removed completely from the home country

Obviously, each of these approaches will have its own quirks. As we move from top to bottom, we expect to see the cost of the outsource decline, although this decline is not always the case. Also, as we move down the list, management of the outsource becomes increasingly problematic. We are going from in-house work to the other side of the planet. Luckily, high-quality technical people exist all over the world so some of the difficulties may be more perceived than real.

We anticipate a move toward distributed teams for noncore functions of enterprises. For example, we can see outsourcing and, perhaps, offshore work for

- Accounting
- Human resources
- Purchasing
- Logistics
- Information technology
- Subcontracted manufacturing work
- Product testing
- Software development

Some of these functions are what we call "generic" functions. The term "generic" is not meant to be an insult. A generic function is an activity where sufficient regulation exists so that the tasks performed by that function are similar regardless of location; that is, these functions are ripe for outsourcing. Of course, if any one of the listed functions is a core activity, it is not a generic activity. The heart of the question for the enterprise is to determine which functions are core activities and which are not, and to see if a cost-effective outsourcing solution is available. Sometimes, the outsource provider will be more competent than the insourced solution simply because the contractor focuses on their specific segment of the business.

Where do consultants fall in this stew of multiple departments, outsourcing, and other approaches? In many cases, the presence of the consultant will be on-site for at least part of the time. If they are on-site for a sufficient duration, the consultant can be a scrum team member. This membership will depend on whether the consultant is expected to remain as an outside, impartial observer or whether they have full participation in the day to day activities of the client. We feel it would be counterproductive to put the consultant on the spot. Furthermore, they may be so expensive that it makes no sense to put them on the scrum team! However, the option to use a consultant on a scrum team is always available.

12.2 Tools for Distributed Teams

In order for a highly distributed (multiple time zone) scrum team to function, they must have tools that allow for communication and some level of control. We have used some of these tools and we are writing this book as a distributed team. Examples of some tools are the following:

- Audio
  - Skype
  - Microsoft Office Communicator
- Audiovisual
  - Skype (in video mode)
  - Microsoft Live Meeting
  - Gotomeeting.com
  - Drake Picture Talk
- Storage
  - Amazon Elastic Compute Cloud
  - Microsoft Sharepoint
- Change control
  - Subversion client and server
  - Git
- Build software (if software development is our product)
  - Make, a scripting tool
  - Ant, scripting tool that uses XML
  - Electric Cloud's Electric Accelerator
  - Perforce

More tools should be available by the time this book goes to print (for example, *git*, another software build tool), both commercial and open source. Our experience suggests that the tool is usually less important than the speed of the connection. Slow lines make meaningful discourse trying. Inexpensive and small laptop computers called "Netbooks" are becoming available. They usually consist of a small keyboard/screen, a light version of the operating system, and 100 to 200 Gigabytes of storage as a hard drive, with everything else hooked up through USB ports. These units are designed to be portable and do most of their work hooked into the Internet. This approach makes more sense than trying to carry on a network conversation using a PDA or a smart phone.

12.3 Drawbacks to Outsourced Scrum

Some of the issues we categorize as drawbacks would apply to traditional program management as well as to the scrum approach. However, we have seen mitigation of some of these issues through the tight control provided by the sprints and the daily scrum meeting and the benefits of network technology.

Some individuals may find it hard to believe, but we have found that time zone problems become a serious issue when dealing with distributed teams (see Figure 12.1). The issue can become even more pronounced when we are trying to have meaningful scrum meetings *every day* and the times are extremely inconvenient for some team members. One of us had to work with a supplier in Singapore while we were in a Texas location. The timing put the Singapore people well into the evening. Your other author has had frequent communication with a Swedish truck

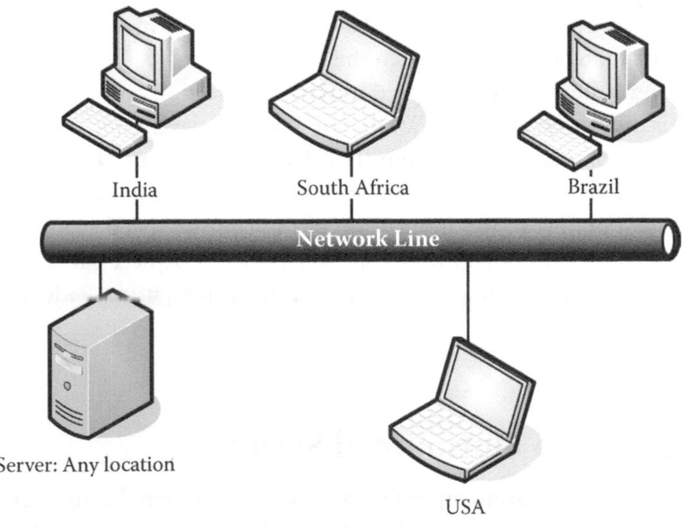

Figure 12.1 Distributed team.

manufacturer—the timing is not nearly as bad between the east coast of the United States and Sweden, but the meetings still take planning. Also, the electronic tools may become impressively slow when dealing with extended distances.

In order to practice a meaningful scrum meeting, we would want to see prompt response from team members; in short, we don't want the technology slowing them down. If we have already established the payback in performance from using the scrum approach locally, we may be able to justify the use of speedier connections.

Another potential downside lies with language issues. We have both worked with parts of our companies that lie outside the United States. Communication can be difficult when all parties speak, for example, English, but it becomes much worse when dealing with non-native speakers, regardless of which direction we are going. We have seen people take off on tasks thinking they were performing correctly, only to discover later that a key word means something completely different (one of the most common is the Spanish word *embarazado*—English-speakers think it means the cognate "embarrassed," but it actually means "pregnant"). Even when the common language is English, the various accents may cause misunderstanding. English, in particular, is difficult to spell and often gives non-native speakers difficulties with pronunciation. Even among European languages, we see substantial variation in the use of prepositions, location of modifiers, and extra tenses.

In some cases, parts of the distributed team may not have the same tool set. For example, one set of members might be using a product like CATIA for computer-aided design and another part of the team might be using Pro-Engineer. Translation between products is not always clean. Some software products may not be available to team members of non-United States countries for security reasons; at other times, tools may not be available because of cost. In India, for example, the Linux operating system is more common than in the United States not only because it is free, but because it is powerful and they do not have the history or investment in Microsoft Windows that many industries have in the United States.

Something as simple as a high-speed Internet connection can cause so much delay that video is out of the question. While not always a developing nations problem, it is more common in developing countries than in Europe or North America. The team should use the fastest connection they have, which may mean that wireless is out of the question due to the attenuation of the transfer speed as more people log on to the router. A video image of the speaker may not be necessary, but display of documents and movies of failures are beneficial (not to mention, reducing the need for expensive travel).

12.4 Upsides to Outsourced Scrum

One major upside to outsourcing is the expansion of potential team members. The enterprise can go quickly from a relatively small local team to a worldwide team, with the attendant potential for enhanced and specialized skill sets. For example,

India is noted for having Capability Maturity Model firms at level five, the highest achievable.

Another upside may be the reduction in cost of staffing, particularly when team members hail from less affluent economies; for example, Mexico or India. We suggest that product quality should be foremost, but the costing imperative makes a great deal of sense, particularly when the skills available in the less affluent economy rival or exceed those available locally or regionally.

The time zone issue can be a gift as well as an impediment. The variety of time zones allows one part of the team to be working on the project while other parts sleep. The daily scrum meeting is essential to keep the work synchronized. A good product data management system or product life cycle management system can assist in this regard. At a minimum, team members should be using a common bucket; for example, a Sharepoint portal. With Skype, the team members can do a primitive level of conferencing (as of this writing); with a product like Microsoft Live Meeting, the team members can hear each other, see each other (with Webcams), and display spreadsheets and other documents on the desktop. Of course, a high-speed line makes this approach a whole lot more pleasant!

We would like to note that sometimes the distant team members are actually closer to our client or customer. We can send the outsource instead of using expensive airplane flights to travel to meetings, reviews, and other interactions. If the team member is also a resident at a customer site, the customer visit is a given. The trick with this approach is to ensure that the resident individual takes part in the daily meetings and the sprint activities. As we have seen repeatedly in this book, the heart of the scrum approach lies with the backlogs and the meeting model—intense, high-speed, very-focused, and flexible.

12.5 Outsourcing—The Future

We suspect that by combining the outsourcing we know will continue to grow with the advantages of the scrum approach, most enterprises will have a winning system. One of the critical factors for expansion of the scrum approach into outsourcing of any kind is the need for high-speed communications, particularly if the addition of video is helpful. The team should have the use of video whiteboards, clean sound, and real-time or nearly real-time video. We don't think it is really necessary to give the illusion that the team is in the same room by using large, high-definition screens, but it is a nice touch.

We believe that the enhanced control derived from frequent quasi-formal reviews and the daily scrum meeting brings a necessary feedback mechanism into the world of outsourcing. One of the most common complaints we have heard over the years occurs when contractors and other augmented teams have been mismanaged. In these cases, we already know that the product backlog clarifies the overall scope, the sprints clarify the immediate scope, and the daily scrum meetings help to keep everything on track as well as provide an early warning system for impending fiascos. For even more control, we can add the burndown charts to graphically represent progress against the sprint plan.

The management of the future should stand back enough from the fray to see if they can observe the *emergence* of real teams. Often, when teams appear, they are emergent phenomena rather than a designated collective. From our own experience, we know that teams that form spontaneously are far more productive than those put together by a manager—concocted in the abstract. An emergent team is an entity with which we work, not something that management works *on*. Like the architect of an apartment building site, we want to leave out the sidewalks until we know where people will create natural paths in the grass and only *then* lay down the sidewalks. Every time we work with people rather than over them, we increase our leverage because we decrease the amount of effort needed to move the group in the desired direction.

Chapter 13

The New Age

In this chapter, we discuss some advanced issues for use by the scrum teams and the associated managers.

13.1 Improvisation

As employees' skills mature, they will proceed through a sequence that resembles that of the medieval and rennaissance guilds: apprentice, journeyman, and master. Of course, we could define a more complex model, but this historic approach is easy to understand. Nor do we claim that the apprentice-journeyman-master approach is particularly efficient—it is just a model representing levels of skills.

13.1.1 Apprentice

The apprentice is an individual who is only beginning to learn the business. At the very beginning, the apprentice may receive training only from the journeyman, if a qualified one is available. We do not feel that an apprentice in our definition is really a protégé; that is, the confidant/advisee of a mentor. In our approach, the apprentice is most definitely being indoctrinated/trained into a new set of skills.

13.1.2 Journeyman

The journeyman is a person who understands the rules for producing a product. Journeymen have internalized the rules and are capable of producing competent products. As we have seen, they have some responsibility for training the apprentices.

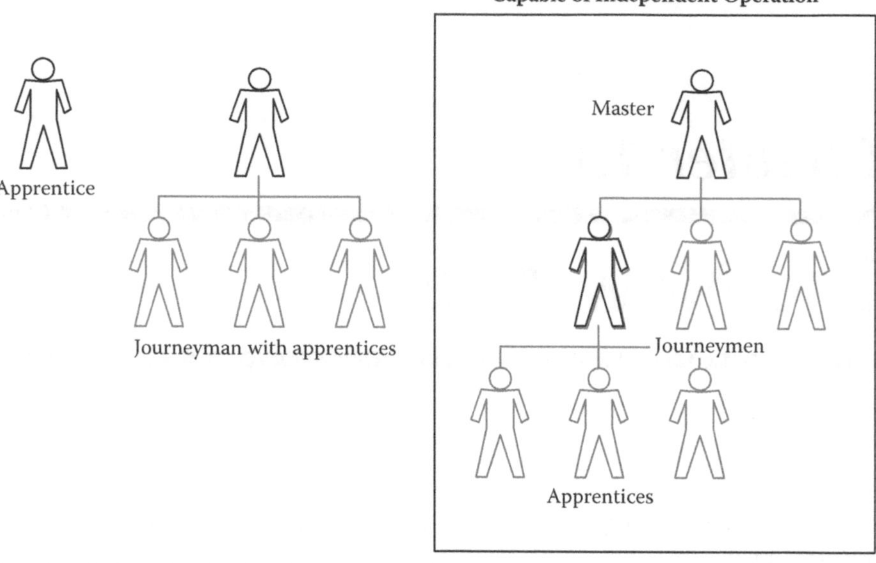

Figure 13.1 Guild relations.

13.1.3 Master

The master is capable of more than producing a competent product. They and their knowledge and skills have become one. It is at the level of mastery that we can expect meaningful improvisation to occur. At the level of the master, project management and functional activities behave more like music or dance than they do like a machine. The master becomes a facilitator for the processes, products, and people to assume their natural rhythms; in short, the master works with systems rather than on or against systems (see Figure 13.1).

Like jazz, this kind of improvisation requires a high level of technical competency and a more qualitative term like "feel." The master has already made 5,000 mistakes and corrected them and has accomplished all the deliberate practice necessary to wed with the function itself. The master will know that the best kind of flow is not the smooth flow of laminar movement but much closer to the edge of chaos.

With regard to improvisation, M.J. Ryan says that she is " . . . suggesting that we get more in tune with the spirit of improvisation, which is all about working with what shows up and not seeing mistakes as mistakes, but as the next thing to riff off of."[1]

13.1.4 Improvisation and Scrum

Because the scrum approach uses high-intensity, cadence-enhancing techniques, it makes for a useful tool for the advanced journeyman and the master. That is not to say that lesser-skilled individuals cannot benefit from the various tools but, rather, that the scrum approach still has value even at the highest levels of attainment.

Because scrum allows for quick course corrections, it is well-suited to improvisational management processes.

In the organizations with which we have worked, we usually see procedure piled on procedure, rule piled on rule, and much heavy-handed bullying of employees in attempts to get them to do what some exalted manager thinks they should be doing. In a situation where we can allow a master to improvise, the processes and products themselves will "speak" and set the tone for subsequent activities. People who are aware of this phenomenon will be heard to say "the process will do what the process will do"—not a fatalistic throwing-up of hands but a realization that without profound knowledge of the process, most changes will be little more than tampering and will ultimately damage the process rather than improve it. Again, M.J. Ryan describes the situation well:

> When we adopt the spirit of improv, the action, evaluation, and respond process goes quickly because we don't spend time in indecision ("Should I do it?"); rumination ("Why can't or won't I do it?"); or regret ("Oh, I just blew it."). We just do and keep on doing, responding to the bounce back we get. The key is to adjust based on the feedback—don't get caught in the trap of continuing to do the same thing expecting different results.[2]

13.2 Emergent Phenomena

We have already made some comments about emergent phenomena. We typically use the term "emergence" when the sum of the parts exceeds the individual total of the values of those parts; in short, we see something that didn't exist when we were dealing with only the parts (see Figure 13.2). A highly functioning team demonstrates emergence as members compensate for the inadequacies of other members in a "dance of balance." Additionally, as trust develops, constituencies break down and the team becomes its own constituency. The kind of trust we see on a really good team is not a blind trust but, rather, a trust in what each member can do, will do, and does. We can infer an emergent phenomenon when we see through testing that the interaction effects are significant and, in some cases, actually outdo the so-called main effects. When dealing with people, we expect interaction effects because they are the very nature of the transaction. Consequently, we see opportunities for emergence as teams mature.

Examples of emergent phenomena occur with societal behavior; biological examples are

- Roving colonies such as army ants
- Termite societies
- Slime molds
- Bird flocks

While some scientists have belittled the concept of emergence, we suspect real emergence is more than just a convenient name for group behavior. Given our reference to

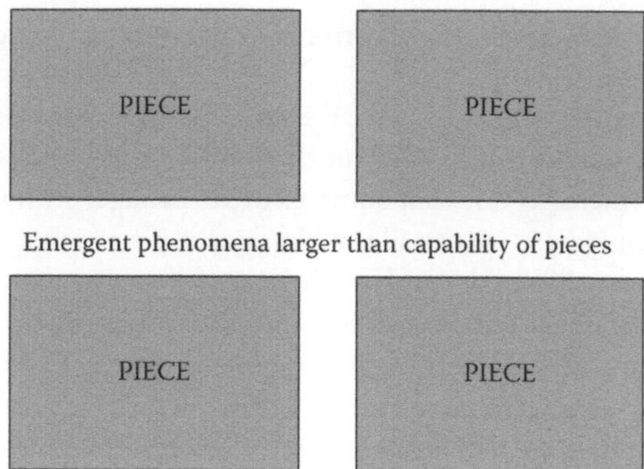

Figure 13.2 Emergent phenomena relations.

significant interactions, we believe emergent phenomena are far more common than generally perceived. What about breakdown of emergence? The breakdown of this effect can occur when a group becomes so large communication becomes difficult and trust relationships suffer. The so-called Dunbar number is approximately 150, which is the number of stable relationships a given individual can maintain. The small team sizes in the scrum approach never get close to the Dunbar value.

13.3 Creative Problem-Solving

When performing creative problem-solving, we sometimes need to move beyond the simplistic approaches seen in manufacturing environments

- The five whys (see Figure 13.3)
- The eight disciplines (8D) (see Figure 13.4)
- Six Sigma: define, measure, analyze, improve, and control (DMAIC)

If a given problem is amenable to a solution using one of these approaches, then, by all means, make use of the technique. However, we need to keep in mind that simple solutions are often good only for simple problems and not every problem will be simple. What follows are some examples of the simpler approaches.

Additionally, we have observed that numerous groups go through a ritual that might be called "rush to solution" or "jump to conclusions," frequently recognizable from excited shouts of "I know, I know . . . ." How can a team, especially a scrum team, maneuver through the quagmire of assumptions, presuppositions, and hidden agendas?

One approach to creative problem-solving might look like the following:

1. Define the problem.
2. Instigate emergency steps if called for.

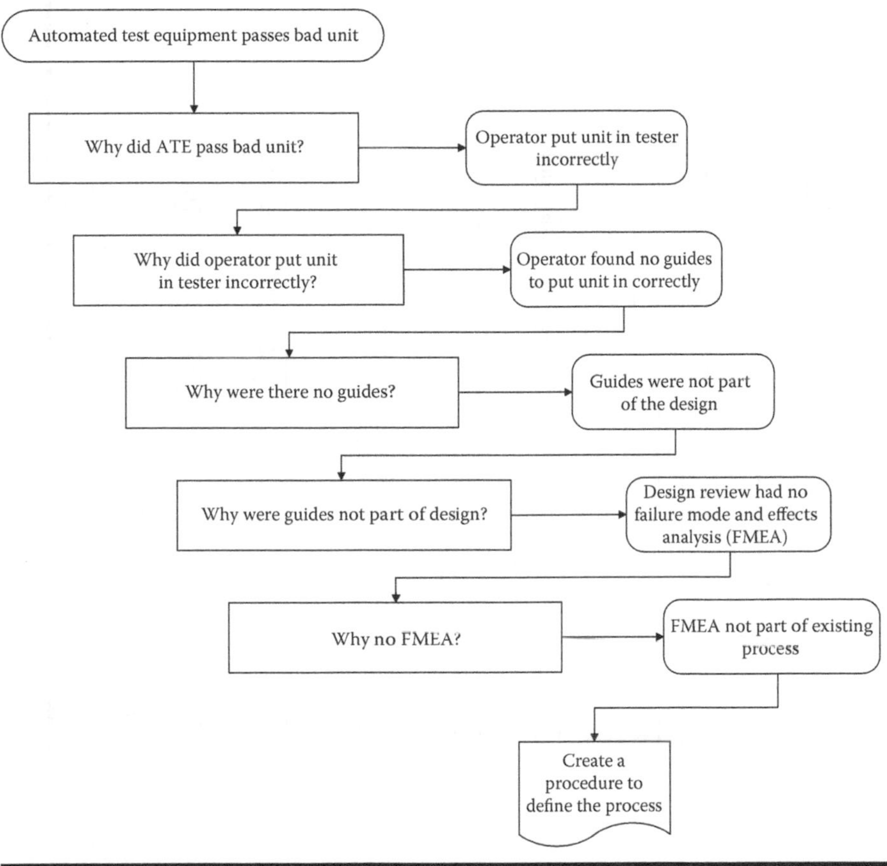

Figure 13.3 Five why problem solving.

3. Identify the scope of the problem.
   a. What is in scope?
   b. What is *not* in scope?
4. Consider containment of the problem.
5. Verify the containment is functioning properly.
6. Identify the root cause.
   a. Beware of reasoning from effects to causes due to the logical fallacy of affirming the consequent!
   b. Look for the synchronic (through time) activities that set up the situation.
   c. Look for the diachronic (cross-section of time) activities that precipitated the situation.
   d. Do *not* leave out candidates.
7. Select a root cause and verify until we believe we have the most likely candidate.
8. Implement a corrective action against this root cause.

8D Report *<title of report>*

Who is Affected by the Problem?		Date Open:		8D#:	
Company:	*<customer name>*	Initial Response:		Customer Complaint Number:	
Location:		Target Close Date:			
Prod Name:		Revision Date(s):			
Part No./Code		8D Initiator:			
	☐ Internal or ☐ External	Actual Close Date:			
D1 – Form Team					
Champion:	*<put in name of 8D champion>*	Team Leader:	*<name of team leader>*		
Team Members:					
D2a – Problem Statement/Description					
D2b – Customer Impact					
D3 – Choose and Verify Interim Containment Action(s) (ICA)				Target Date:	Actual Date:
How Did You Verify the Effectiveness of the ICA?					
D4 – Define and Verify Root Cause(s)					
How Did You Verify the Root Cause(s)?					
D5 – Choose and Verify Permanent Corrective Action(s) (PCA)					
How Did You Verify the Effectiveness of the PCA?					
D6 – Implement and Validate Permanent Corrective Action(s)				Target Date:	Actual Date:
How Will You Validate the PCA?					
D7 – Actions to Prevent Recurrence				Target Date:	Actual Date:
Has corrective action/implementation been reviewed against documents? Check boxes that apply: ☐ Lessons Learned ☐ Design Checklist ☐ Process/Procedure ☐ Generic Spec ☐ FMEA ☐ Control Plan ☐ Add to Internal Audit					
D8 – Congratulate the Team					

Figure 13.4 8D generic format.

9. Consider implementing corrective actions against the other candidates if this is feasible and economical.
10. Perform an after-action review.
11. Log the history of this situation in the lessons learned database.
12. If using failure mode and effects analyses (FMEA), record information there as well.
13. Set up a refresher schedule for training/indoctrinating the project staff on known issues.

The lessons learned update, the FMEA, and the training are critical to institutionalizing the solution to this situation. We have seen teams add information to the lessons learned database and find out later that the database has become a graveyard for critical information. It is also important to consider the measurement system used to detect any issues. If the measurement system is flawed, the team will not see the issue until it is too late. A scrum team is lightweight enough to consider revisions of the measurement system improved such that it will flag issues as they arise.

Notes

1. M.J. Ryan, *AdaptAbility*, (New York, NY: Broadway Books, 2009), 172
2. M.J. Ryan, *AdaptAbility*, (New York, NY: Broadway Books, 2009), 173

Chapter 14

Final Words

We view the scrum approach to any kind of project management as a "small loop" methodology. Those of us with a quality engineering background will see the daily scrum meetings and short range sprints as instantiations of the plan-do-check-act (PDCA) Shewhart (or Deming) Circle. We were gratified to see an excellent discussion of the small loop approach in Mike Rother's book, *Toyota Kata*.

We have no intention of promoting scrum in the religious sense often seen with flavors of the week like Six Sigma and lean manufacturing. We are suggesting that the reader look at the approach, try it out, and see what works. We have been successful with the approach, particularly with test engineering. We have found it to be more difficult to launch with managers who prefer to "wing it" in their operations. We suspect that these less-structured managers wouldn't be any happier with the traditional approach, although they may be more proficient at hiding their sins due to their more complete understanding of the traditional methods and reporting schemes. In our experience, shoot-from-the-hip managers prefer to work in isolation so they can avoid the critiques that are likely to occur were they are under observation.

Scrum is less a panacea than a *simple method for accelerating the drum beat of accomplishment in the workplace.* Frequent, short team meetings help forge real teams rather than appointed pseudo-teams, driving home the idea of common interest and accomplishment. Information is never more than about a day old and flows freely between at least two levels. Cascading approaches such as scrum of scrums, not surprisingly, require more management and the flow of information can get stifled among multiple levels—although it should still flow well between two contiguous levels.

We find that employees like the short, regular meetings instead of the infrequent marathons to which they were invited, using the more traditional approach. Even the biweekly or monthly sprint meetings are well-contained and represent an improvement over the ultra-marathons used previously. We have seen some resistance in two areas: using the burndown charts and building a good enough work breakdown structure to populate the product backlogs and thence the sprint backlogs. In some cases, we have forced the issue to get the staff to at least try the approach out, knowing full well that once they saw it work, they would become true believers. Once your team believes they can increase their pace without increasing their suffering, they become energized. It doesn't hurt them to see the never-ending action-item list begin to shrivel away as more and more projects are completed. The use of micro-tasks derived from a comprehensive and detailed work breakdown structure provides a list of relatively easy-to-complete activities that constantly reinforces the sense of movement and accomplishment.

The sense of achievement and the possibilities for daily recognition from the team leader comprise two of the items in Frederick Herzberg's motivators (non-hygienic factors): achievement, recognition, the work in and of itself, responsibility, promotions (form of recognition), and growth. Of course, the hygienic factors are important if missing, but it is interesting to see how observed behaviors dovetail with Herzberg's motivational theory.

Another point we would like to make is the importance of the work breakdown structure. This document should be taken to the utmost detail regardless of whether we are using conventional project management or the scrum approach. We call this breaking the tasks down to the "atomic" level, the level beyond which it no longer makes any sense to break an item down. The extremely fine resolution makes it much easier to calculate disposition to team members as well as to the "extended family." Tasks are now either complete or incomplete, a binary proposition. If we are using a tool like Microsoft Project, we can fill in either 0% or 100% for the binary condition and let the software do the roll-up to calculate the percentage complete for that group of tasks—a nice feature when management wants an idea of project status in the form of percentage complete. Those readers familiar with manufacturing terminology might consider the work breakdown structure to be a form of the bill of process.

In some cases, we can take the work breakdown structure and construct simple checklists out of a select grouping of items. These checklists are functionally equivalent to the sprint backlogs and the higher order versions are analogs of the product backlogs. We can now see why we consider the work breakdown structure to be the *heart* of project management, regardless of style. The work breakdown structure is the one essential document in all of project management.

John Boyd was a U.S. Air Force colonel who researched why U.S. pilots in Korea were able to shoot down North Korean pilots, who had better aircraft initially. He observed:

> The idea of fast transients suggests that, in order to win, we should operate at a faster tempo or rhythm than our adversaries, or better yet, get inside our adversary's observation-orientation-decision-action time cycle or loop.[1]

We maintain that increasing tempo also increases our competitive edge. It does so in the following ways:

- We increase our time for "wiggle room" when things go amiss.
- Jobs are generally completed sooner.
- Visibility of negative issues increases.
- A customer can be informed of progress frequently.

Note

1. John R. Boyd, *Patterns of Conflict*, (1981), http://www.d-n-i.net/Patterns of conflict original.pdf (accessed 15 October 2009)

Bibliography

The Institute of Electrical and Electronics Engineers, Inc. *IEEE Std 1061–1998, IEEE Standard for a Software Quality Metrics Methodology.* New York, NY, April 1999.

The Institute of Electrical and Electronics Engineers, Inc. *IEEE Std 1028–1997, IEEE Standard for a Software Reviews.* New York, NY, April 1999.

Bellman, G.M. *Getting Things Done When You Are Not in Charge.* New York, NY: Fireside, 2001.

Berry, Tim. *The Plan-As-You-Go Business Plan.* Canada: Entreprenuer Media, Inc., 2008.

Blanchard, Kenneth and Lorber, Robert. *Putting the One Minute Manager to Work.* New York, NY: Berkley, 1984.

Bridges, W. *The Way of Transition: Embracing Life's Most Difficult Moments.* Reading, MA: Perseus, 2001.

Boyd, John R. *Patterns of Conflict.* (1981) `http://www.d-n-i.net/Patterns of conflict original.pdf` (accessed 15 October 2009).

Chawla, S. and Renesch, J. *Learning Organizations: Developing Cultures for Tomorrow's Workplace (1st ed.).* Portland, OR: Productivity Press, 1995.

Chrissis, Mary Beth, Konrad, Mike, and Shrum, Sandy. *CMMI Guidelines for Process Integration and Product Improvement.* Boston, MA: Addison-Wesley, 2003.

Cohn, Mike. *Agile Estimating and Planning.* New York, NY: Prentice Hall Professional Technical Reference, 2006.

Cohn, Mike. *User Stories Applied, For Agile Software Development.* New York, NY: Addison Wesley, 2004.

Cooke, Helen S. and Tate, Karen. *36 Hour Course in Project Management.* New York, NY: McGraw-Hill, 2006.

Corley, R.N., Reed, O.L., Shedd, P.J., and Morehead, J.W. *The Legal and Regulatory Environment of Business (12th ed.).* Homewood, IL: Irwin/McGraw-Hill, 2002.

Creating Teams with an Edge. Boston, MA: Harvard Business School Press, 2004.

Derby, Esther and Larsen, Diana. *Agile Retrospectives: Making Good Teams Great.* Raleigh, NC: The Pragmatic Bookself, 2006.

Discoe, Paul. *Zen Architecture: The Building Process as Practice.* Layton, UT: Gibbs Smith, 2008.

Dunbar, R.I.M. (1993). "Coevolution of neocortical size, group size and language in humans." *Behavioral and Brain Sciences* 16 (4). Cambridge, UK: Cambridge Unviverity Press, 1993.

Eisenberg, E.M. and Goodall, H.L. *Organizational Communication: Balancing Creativity and Constraint (2nd ed.).* New York, NY: St. Martin's Press, 1997.

Ferris, Timothy. *The 4-Hour Workweek.* New York, NY: Crown Publishing, 2007.

Fisher, Kimball. *Leading Self-Directed Work Teams, A Guide to Developing New Team Leadersip Skills.* New York, NY: McGraw-Hill, 1993.

Fleming, Q.W. and Koppelman, J.M. *Earned Value Project Management. Project Management Institute (2nd ed.).* Newtown Square, PA: PMI®, 2000.

Gharajedaghi, J. *Systems Thinking: Managing Chaos and Complexity.* Woburn, MA: Butterworth-Heinemann, 1999.

Grenning, James. (2002) *Planning Poker,* http:www.objectmentor.comresourcesarticlesPlanning Poker.zip, retrieved 29 December 2009.

Guffey, Mary Ellen. *Essentials of Business Communication (6th ed).* Independence, KY: Thomson South-Western, 2003.

Heldman, Kim. *Project Managers: Spotlight on Risk Management.* San Francisco, CA: Harbor Light Press, 2005.

Heneman, H.G. III, Heneman, R.L., and Judge, T.A. *Staffing Organizations (2nd ed.).* Middleton, WI: Mendota House, Irwin, 1997.

Herzberg, Frederick. *The Motivation to Work,* New York, NY: John Wiley & Sons, 1959.

Hesselbein, F., Goldsmith, M., and Beckhard, R. *The Leader of the Future: New Visions, Strategies, and Practices for the Next Era. The Drucker Foundation—Future Series.* San Francisco, CA: Josey-Bass Publishers, 1996.

CH2M Hill Project Managers. *Project Delivery: A System and Process for Benchmark Performance (4th ed.).* Denver, CO: Author, 2001.

Katzenbach, John R. *The Wisdom of Teams.* New York, NY: HarperCollins Publishers, 1993.

Kerzner, H. *Project Management: A Systems Approach to Planning, Scheduling, and Controlling (7th ed.).* New York, NY: John Wiley & Sons, 2001.

Larman, Craig. *Agile & Iterative Development; A Managers Guide.* New York, NY: Addison-Wesley McGraw-Hill, 2004.

Lewis, J.P. *Project Planning, Scheduling and Control (3rd ed.).* New York, NY: McGraw-Hill, 2000.

Meredith, J.R. and Mantel, S.J., Jr. *Project Management: A Managerial Approach (4th ed.).* New York, NY: John Wiley & Sons, 2000.

Phillips, Donald T. *Lincoln on Leadership, Executive Strategies for Tough Times.* New York, NY: Warner Books, 1992.

Poppendieck, Tom. (2003) *The Agile Customer's Toolkit.* http:www.poppendieck.compdfs/ Agile_Customers_Toolkit_Paper.pdf accessed 16 June, 2009.

Rother, Mike. *Toyota Kata: Managing People for Improvement, Adaptiveness, and Superior Results.* New York, NY: McGraw-Hill, 2010.

Ryan, M.J. *AdaptAbility.* New York, NY: Broadway Books, 2009.

Schwaber, Ken. *The Enterprise and Scrum.* Redmond, WA: MicroSoft Press, 2007.

Schwaber, Ken, and Beedle, Mike. *Agile Software Development with Scrum.* Upper Saddle River, NJ: Prentice Hall, 2002.

Senge, P. *The Fifth Discipline: The Art and Practice of the Learning Organization.* New York, NY: Doubleday-Currency, 1994.

Senge, P., Roberts, C., Ross, R.B., Smith, B.J., and Kleiner, A. *The Fifth Discipline Fieldbook: Strategies and Tools for Building a Learning Organization.* New York, NY: Doubleday-Currency, 1994.

Shannon, Claude E. "A Mathematical Theory of Communication." *Bell System Technical Journal,* 27, 379, 623, July and October, 1948.

Stepanek, George. *Software Project Secrets. Why Software Projects Fail.* New York, NY: Apress, 2005.

Verzuh, E. *The Fast Forward MBA in Project Management.* New York, NY: John Wiley & Sons, 1999.

Wideman, R. M. (Ed.) *Project and Program Risk Management: A Guide to Managing Project Risks and Opportunities.* Newtown, PA: Project Management Institute, 1992.

Index

S

T

W